D0880426

Unleashing the Power of Intercessory Prayer

Joseph Hollcraft

Unleashing the Power of Intercessory Prayer

SOPHIA INSTITUTE PRESS

Manchester, New Hampshire

Copyright © 2020 by Joseph Hollcraft

Printed in the United States of America. All rights reserved.

Cover by LUCAS Art & Design, Jenison, MI, in collaboration
with Perceptions Design Studio.

Cover image: *The Coronation of the Virgin*, ca.1440,
by Fra Angelico (XAL49984) © Bridgeman Images.

Unless otherwise noted, Scripture quotations in this work are taken from the
Revised Standard Version of the Bible: Catholic Edition, copyright © 1965, 1966 the
Division of Christian Education of the National Council of the Churches of Christ
in the United States of America, and are used by permission of the copyright
owner. All rights reserved. Quotations marked "NABRE" are taken from the
New American Bible, revised edition © 2010, 1991, 1986, 1970 Confraternity of
Christian Doctrine, Washington, D.C. Used by permission. All rights reserved.
No part of the *New American Bible* may be reproduced in any form without per-
mission in writing from the copyright owner.

Excerpts from the English translation of the *Catechism of the Catholic Church*,
second edition, © 1994, 1997, 2000 by Libreria Editrice Vaticana–United States
Conference of Catholic Bishops, Washington, D.C. All rights reserved.

No part of this book may be reproduced, stored in a retrieval system, or transmitted
in any form, or by any means, electronic, mechanical, photocopying, or otherwise,
without the prior written permission of the publisher, except by a reviewer, who
may quote brief passages in a review.

Sophia Institute Press
Box 5284, Manchester, NH 03108
1-800-888-9344

www.SophiaInstitute.com

Sophia Institute Press® is a registered trademark of Sophia Institute.

Paperback ISBN 978-1-64413-338-5
eBook ISBN 978-1-64413-339-2
Library of Congress Control Number: 2020942352

Second printing

To my wife, Jackie, with love and gratitude

In memoriam of Joseph Hollcraft, my nephew,
who trod the path of humility

Contents

Foreword

During my hospitalization for COVID-19, I agreed to participate in a clinical trial to test a treatment that could be effective for those suffering from the virus. During my last visit to the clinic, they drew about eight vials of blood and asked me several questions. As we were talking, the nurse revealed that two other patients had agreed to the trial at the same time. I was saddened to learn that one of those patients died (God rest his soul) and the other was still in the hospital. The nurse was encouraged that they had at least one patient who had survived. For perspective, the reason that the three of us were in the study together is that we were all high-risk patients with a common, specific underlying issue. Statistically, 80 percent of those who get intubated (go on a ventilator) don't survive. I was on a ventilator. With the underlying issues at play, the death rate is probably much higher, which means I didn't have much of a chance of survival, humanly speaking anyway.

This is important—pay close attention. Yes, it was clearly God's will that I live, and I know that because I am alive. So the outcome that God desired was that I live. However, the means that He used was the cooperation of His people: His will was that they pray for me in order for the ends to come to fruition. Said another way, God's desired end was that I live. His chosen means to achieve that end were the prayers of His people. Here's how Saint Thomas Aquinas puts it in the *Summa*:

> We pray, not that we may change the divine decree, but that we may impetrate that which God has decreed to be fulfilled by our prayers.[1]

So then, what happens when you don't pray?

If you don't cooperate with God and intercede when called to do so, the graces that should have come through your "yes" are blocked by your "no." Even Jesus was unable to do miracles in His hometown because of unbelief (Matt. 13:58). Unbelief is a "no" to God that stifles our faith and prayer and dries up the grace that God desires to pour out upon us.

This is why, when someone says, "I prayed for you," I respond, "Thank you. I am alive because you prayed, and God answered your prayers." Every time I say it, I mean it from the depths of my being, and I mean it specifically as it relates to the "yes" of that person.

With your prayers, God will move and achieve His ends. Without them, far less grace will rain down on those who need it. Without your prayers, the Church will continue to slide into apostasy, and many will perish without knowing Jesus. With your prayers, your reparation, your repentance, we can and will be revived and renewed.

—Dan Burke
President, Avila Institute

[1] *ST* II-II, 83, 2c.

Preface

In May of 2017, SpiritualDirection.com posted an article of mine titled "12 Points to Consider When Praying for Others." Over the following days, I received numerous prayer requests along with many general comments in my inbox. Due to the overwhelming response, I flirted with the idea of expanding the article into a book. As time passed and interest grew, flirting turned into a full-blown relationship in the form of the book that you now hold in your hands.

In the writing of this book, the twelve points became nine keys, and the nine keys were then expanded in their practical and theological scopes. Each chapter now offers tips on how to pray according to each key and explores the *why* behind each one.

I have multiple reasons for writing this book. First, I hope that you come to understand praying for others as a vital expression of the Christian faith. Second, I hope that you internalize intercessory prayer not as something you have to do, but as something you want and are privileged to do. Third, I want to provide a resource to turn to as you seriously take up this vocation to pray for others. In order to accomplish these goals, I designed a structure to help you along the way. Each chapter focuses on an intercessory key, explains practical tips, discusses a key patron saint, and provides prompt questions for journaling. After the last chapter, I include a recommended prayer for intercession composed by Saint Margaret Mary Alacoque. Every saint in the Catholic Church has a God-given power to intercede on behalf of man and the Church (see Rev. 5:8; 8:3–5). I have paired up a saint with each key so that we might draw strength and wisdom from their witnesses in our calling to pray for others.

Lastly, I hope that through the practice of intercessory prayer you find yourself desiring more of God in your daily walk, for with every Christian topic explored, there is more reason to love God.

I do not assert these nine keys as the "be all, end all" response to the question "Will you pray for me?" But I can testify that when I have said, "Yes, I will pray for you," these keys, under God's grace, have enriched my prayer immensely!

Acknowledgments

I want to first thank Dr. Anthony Lilles for his encouragement early in the writing process and his willingness to pick up the phone anytime I had a question. Also, to Bob Sutton, Jacqueline Hollcraft (sister-in-law), and Regis Flaherty for their editing and advice.

I extend a sincere thanks to the team at Sophia Institute Press for their involvement in bringing this book to its conclusion, especially Angie Allen. Her constructive feedback was invaluable to the maturation of this work.

Additionally, I extend a warm thanks to Dan Burke, for his engaging foreword and testament to the power of intercessory prayer.

I thank those closest to me, whose many conversations gave shape to the words in this book, most especially Father Blaise Berg and Deacon Ray Helgeson. And to Sister Victoria Maria of the Infant King Jesus, O.C.D. (my sister), whose daily prayers of intercession helped sustain me during this work—I love you!

Lastly, and most importantly, I express my gratitude to my beautiful children: Kolbe, Avila, Isaac, and Siena, for the many joys they brought to me while I wrote this book.

—Joseph Hollcraft
July 16, 2020
Feast of Our Lady of Mount Carmel

Introduction

I had the opportunity to go on a short road trip with my father a few months before he passed away. During that trip, he told me of an important encounter he'd had with a local priest, Father Ron, in 1984.

"Why was it so important?" I asked.

My dad responded, "Do you remember what was going on in 1984?"

"Yes. You and mom were apart."

"Yes, and that is why it was so important," my father said emphatically. He continued, "On a Saturday afternoon, after Father Ron had heard my confession, he asked me, 'What more can I do for you, Bob?' I said to him, 'There is only one thing left: Will you pray for me?'" Father Ron responded, 'Yes, you can count on my prayers!'"

As it turns out, my dad had many follow-up visits with Father Ron, and Father Ron always assured him of his prayers. Soon thereafter, my dad would return to my mom. After relocation, and with much healing grace, the Hollcraft family was set back on the path of prayer and aspiring holiness.

Many things contributed to this turn of events for my family. Still, I firmly believe that all those "things" were made possible by the power of intercessory prayer, primarily the supplication of Father Ron.

Unleashing the Power of Intercessory Prayer

"Will you pray for me?" These five words, when strung together, form one of the most critical questions in the spiritual life. How we respond to this question can change the course of someone's life, and as such, the course of history—as it did for the Hollcraft family. More globally, because someone prayed for Anjezë Gonxhe Bojaxhiu, God unleashed Saint Mother Teresa of Calcutta upon the world; because someone prayed for Karol Wojtyla, God unleashed Saint John Paul II upon the world; because you pray for the person God is calling you to pray for, God will unleash the next saint upon the world. Intercessory prayer is that powerful and that important! God has an end in mind—the revelation of His glory and the salvation of man. Our intercessory prayer helps bring about this end. Without intercessory prayer, there would be less glory revealed and fewer souls saved.

Now where do we start? Unfortunately, many folks struggle with intercessory prayer because they lack a coherent understanding of what prayer *is* and *how* to pray. So, first off, what is prayer?

Prayer is "an elevation of mind and heart to God" (see CCC 2559). Many of the saints refer to it as conversation with God. In every exchange between two people, someone speaks and another person listens. It is no different with God. Without these necessary components, any conversation, including prayer, breaks down.

In our prayer lives, we are tempted to dislike what we hear, primarily when God responds to our prayers with "no" or "not yet." We tend to allow the conversation to end without turning to Scripture or the writings of the saints to shed light on our seemingly unanswered prayers. Interestingly, as parents, we too say "no" or "not yet" to requests from our children because, from our vantage points, we understand that saying "yes" is not always in a child's best interests at that time. This is precisely how we must understand our prayerful dialogues with God to overcome the selective listening that prevents authentic conversation with Him. Samuel did not say, "Listen, for your servant is speaking," but

"Speak, for your servant is listening" (1 Sam. 3:10). We listen first to understand and then to respond. The listen-response dynamic lies at the heart of all good prayer.

To pray well is to pray in faith, in which the listen-response dynamic is fundamental. My son plays the guitar. Before his lessons, he often tunes his guitar. Guitars are made of wood, and wood expands and contracts due to temperature change, which directly impacts the pitch of the string. For the guitar to serve the purpose for which it was created, to play music well, it needs constant re-tuning. The whole realm of praying in faith is a matter of being in tune with God and recognizing the need for constant retuning of ourselves.

Saint Paul employs a significant phrase for us to better understand faith — "the obedience of faith" (Rom. 1:5; 16:26), which hearkens back to the Old Testament interpretation of faithfulness translated as "responsive listening" (*emunah*). Incidentally, the word "obedience" is derived from the Latin *ob-audire*, which translates as "to listen." Given the nature of obedience, we could say that faith is "listening well," or being in tune with God. Praying in faith is listening well to the *Who* you believe in and responding with acts of love. Saint Paul begins and ends his Letter to the Romans with this central message: obedience that springs from faith is a response of listening.

Conversely, when we fail to listen well, or when we are out of tune with God, our lives become discordant with Him. The Latin for "out of tune; discordant" is *absurdus*, meaning that when we do not listen to God we, quite literally, begin to live "absurd" lives. Ironically, the secular world generally looks upon faith and sees it as absurd. Why? Because the world is out of tune with God. People pay a lot of attention to creation but not to the Creator; they recognize goodness but not the One who is Good. Our culture, which elevates the "rebel" — the person who says "no" to the right things — views the virtue of obedience as either foreign or weak. For the Christian, however, obedience is at the center of his revealed faith. The

Christian follows the example of Christ, who "emptied himself, taking the form of a servant, being born in the likeness of men ... [and] in human form he humbled himself and *became obedient unto death,* even death on a cross" (Phil. 2:7–8). If we wish to harmonize our lives with the life of Christ, we take a good first step in doing so by being obedient—listening well and conforming our lives to the One to whom we listen. Saint Thomas Aquinas is known to have said, "If obedience is lacking, [then] ... prayer cannot be pleasing to God." We cannot have faith-filled prayer without obedience because we cannot obey a voice that we do not hear.

We listen better by "tuning out" the noise of the world, which involves turning down the volume on anything that does not resound God's voice. In a fun play on letters, it appears being silent is inherent to listening well. To L-I-S-T-E-N is to be S-I-L-E-N-T. In the end, the only thing "absurd" for the Christian is when we find ourselves out of tune with God (more on this in chapter 7).

What's more, this prayerful conversation is "constant" (1 Thess. 5:17)—without ceasing. So much can be learned from thinking of our relationships with God in prayer analogously to our human relationships. Going on dates is a formal expression of a couple's love that gives shape to their perpetual courtship. In turn, these formal, concrete experiences foster and promote the informal, unplanned moments together. Both the formal and informal aspects of prayer make possible prayer "without ceasing." Prayer is how we engage in perpetual courtship with God.

For Catholics, the formal aspect of prayer is the Eucharist; it is the high point of our lives because in the reception of the Eucharist we experience union—oneness in body and soul—with Christ. When Jesus said, "It is finished" (John 19:30), He meant, "It is consummated" (*consummatum est*). What is consummated? Our union with Christ in the Eucharist—signed, sealed, and delivered in the blood that spills out from the side of Christ.

The Mass shapes all aspects of our relationship with Christ and envelops, sustains, and gives meaning to all informal moments with the Lord. When we struggle to pray informally, oftentimes the formal prayers of the Church, such as the Mass, popular devotions, the Divine Office, and those prayers that our parents taught us as children, help us to reignite the spontaneous prayer we are neglecting. Liturgical prayer teaches us, most of all, that the Church herself never ceases to pray, and therefore neither should we as individuals. We never "retire" from prayer if we are living a courtship-like relationship with God.[2] Prayer with God is not work from which we retire; it is the most important relationship of our lives. We must devote our attentions and care to it without end.

In prayer, we are drawn into the very life of God — the life in which "the Holy Spirit Himself intercedes for us through wordless groans … according to the will of God" (Rom. 8:26–27; see CCC 2634). Herein lies an important point for us in our reflections on prayer and its relationship with intercession. When we pray, whether for others or for ourselves, the Holy Spirit is always and continually *interceding* for us. In this space, we wait for the Spirit's promptings on how He wants us to pray. This does not exclude God's invitation to "let our requests be made known to God" (Phil 4:6) but always includes God as the protagonist of our prayer. As this book will show, the best intercessory prayer is an outgrowth of union with God: we must first receive His love and mercy before we share in His outgoing love and mercy.

This intercession of the Holy Spirit is made possible by Christ's Incarnation and the Paschal Mystery. By becoming one of us, God sanctifies humanity and makes possible a new participation, a participation in God's very divinity. In Baptism, we become an "adopted son of God … a 'partaker of the divine nature,' member of

---

[2]   This element of prayer was also treated in my first book, *A Heart for Evangelizing* (Steubenville, OH: Emmaus Road, 2016), 9–11.

Christ and co-heir with Him, and a temple of the Holy Spirit" (CCC 1265). Under the grace received in Baptism, all Christian faithful are made holy because they now abide *in* the holiness of God, i.e., in Christ. Saint Paul preferred the phrase "in Christ," as opposed to "Christian," because Baptism is the sacrament of being incorporated into Christ. We are *Christian* to the extent that we abide *in Christ*. Therefore, our intercessory prayer is a *going into* (sharing) the one mediation of Christ.[3]

Incidentally, this helps us better understand the sometimes misinterpreted words of Saint Paul, "For there is one God, and there is one mediator between God and men, the man Christ Jesus" (1 Tim. 2:5). Without context, this verse about there being "one mediator" appears to be at odds with the concept of intercessory prayer, in which we ourselves become mediators between God and one who needs prayer. However, a mediator is simply one who resolves conflict between two parties. Theologically, it is a priest who resolves conflict between God and man (the conflict of sin). Saint Paul refers to Christ as the "one mediator" because He, once and for all, carried out the perfect resolution of the conflict between God and man. As

---

[3] While the words "mediation" and "intercession" are often used interchangeably, there is a formal distinction between the two. A mediator intercedes on behalf of another. He can offer intercession because the one from whom he asks recognizes his authority. As long as the mediator has standing with both parties, he can intercede between them with the power and authority that intercession requires. A mediator bestows favor and intercedes because he has the power to do so. In revelation, the word of choice as the one who goes to intercede is not "intercessor," but "mediator"; intercession is the action. Another distinction ought to be made between petition and intercession. The *Catechism* reminds us, "When we share in God's saving love, we understand that *every need* can become the object of petition" (2633). In turn, "intercession is a prayer of petition which leads us to pray as Jesus did" (CCC 2634).

the God-Man, only He had the ability to do so when He sacrificed Himself on the Cross for the forgiveness of our sins. Therefore, Christ is the "one mediator," the one priest, and the one sacrifice through which man's relationship with God is restored. And yet we are part of the Mystical Body of Christ. We are members of His Church, participating in this great work of redemption by virtue of our Baptism. By our prayers of intercession, we engage in this participation, in this work of redemption, with and through Christ. Only He is the perfect mediator, but we are invited, and called, to share in this work (see 2 Pet. 1:4; Col. 1:24).

Furthermore, Saint Paul's quote can be better understood in its proper context. Just a few verses earlier, Saint Paul was urging prayers of intercession for the salvation of souls: "First of all, then, I urge that supplications, prayers, *intercessions*, and thanksgivings be made for all people.... *This is good and it is acceptable in the sight of God our Savior, who desires all people to be saved* and to come to the knowledge of the truth" (1 Tim. 2:1–4, emphasis added). Saint Paul writes "first" because the priority of the Church and the people of God is to pray. One mode of this prayer is to intercede with the help of the Holy Spirit. For Saint Paul, it is clear—intercessory prayer in the one mediation of Jesus Christ is salvific, and it is something which we are "urged" to carry out.[4]

God gave us the means to achieve His ends, and intercessory prayer is a means, or way, for us to share in His drawing all men to Himself. In intercessory prayer, we do not change God's mind, but we bring what is in God's mind to fruition. God does not need our prayers to act, but He chooses to use our prayers to act—the prayer,

---

[4]   The first prayer of the Church is the Eucharist (the Greek word for thanksgiving in 1 Timothy 2:1 is *eucharistias*), and St. Paul is urging Timothy and his local Church to unite all prayers with the one prayer of the Eucharist. We will explore this detail in chapter 8.

that again, arises from deep union with God. The Greek word for intercession points to the intimate communion one shares with God, whereby the one praying enjoys favor with God to make a request. The Greek also connotes a drawing near to God *with an urgent need* (more on this in chapter 5).

Saint Paul wants us to see that our prayers of intercession are "good and acceptable" in God's presence and that all petitions of intercession find their proper conduit in and through Christ Jesus (see John 15:7–8; Phil. 1:19). Saint Paul was urging intercessory prayers because Christ urged us to go to Him with our prayers of intercession and, by doing so, to share in His power (see Eph. 6:18). We share in His power by the power of the Holy Spirit. The one mediation of Christ is always in the power of the Holy Spirit — for Jesus Christ and the Holy Spirit never act separately.

God wants us to think as He thinks, act as He acts, and live as He lives. Praying for others is a beautiful way of thinking, acting, and living as Christ (see Heb. 7:25). In and through intercessory prayer, God is asking us to enter more deeply into His outgoing love and mercy. Essentially, our intercessory prayer imitates the action of the men who carry their friend to Jesus for healing (see Mark 2:3–5). We are called to act by bringing the needs of others, the needs of our friends, before Jesus. Jesus said, "Bring him to me" (Mark 9:19), and so we do.

This action of intercessory prayer is mutually beneficial. As the nature of a gift is something both given and received, it is always shared by two. Saint Paul urges Timothy to the prayer of supplication and intercession because he wants Timothy to share in the gift of intercessory prayer. This prayer guides the one who is praying in the work of sanctification by *focusing on* and *praying for* the needs of others.

As we set out on the path of better understanding what praying for others means, we will do so in the form of nine keys — each key unveiling God's loving plan to build up His kingdom one prayer at a time.

Pray in the Spirit

I was once in the company of someone I consider to be a very holy man: then-Bishop Chaput (later Archbishop Chaput of Philadelphia). It was early in the morning, and I was invited to pray in his presence. As I entered that space of prayer, I found myself just yards away from him. Initially, it sounded as if he was snoring. As seconds turned into minutes, it dawned on me. He was not falling asleep on God but praying in God—in the Holy Spirit. He wasn't snoring but grunting, moaning, sighing. I suppose the Holy Spirit was inspiring Bishop Chaput with "sighs too deep for words" (Rom. 8:26).

My encounter with the holy man has stayed with me because of its teaching point: the Holy Spirit inspires and brings us into the presence of God. Substantially, "Man achieves the fullness of prayer not when he expresses himself, but when he lets God be most fully present in prayer."[5]

Intercessory Key: Pray in the Spirit

All good prayer starts in the Holy Spirit because the Holy Spirit initiates *the movement of God* in our hearts. The Holy Spirit blows

---

[5]   Pope John Paul II, *Crossing the Threshold of Hope* (New York: Knopf, 1995), 18.

life into our hearts—inspiring and inflaming us with love for God because He is the love of God.[6]

The Holy Spirit has the leading role in the drama that unfolds in our listen-response relationships with God. He awakens within us the desire to encounter God—to talk with Him. The gift of Love—God, the Holy Spirit—desires that we speak with the One who eternally gives love—God the Father. Recall Romans 8:26–27:

> Likewise, the Spirit helps us in our weakness; for we do not know how to pray as we ought, but the Spirit himself intercedes for us with *sighs too deep for words*. And he who searches the hearts of men knows what is the mind of the Spirit, because the Spirit intercedes for the saints according to the will of God.

Praying on behalf of others in the Spirit is to "sigh" and "groan" on behalf of others in the presence of God. "Sighs" and "groans" communicate to God the great care with which we bring our petitions of intercession to Him. When we pray with "sighs" and "groans," according to Saint Paul, we use the very language of the Holy Spirit—the language of love! Therefore, invite the Holy Spirit into your life and allow Him to deepen your intercessory prayer.

---

[6] The phrase "gift of the Holy Spirit" in its Latin construct is a *genitive of identity* as opposed to a *genitive of possession*. In Latin, genitives are used to convey a person's relationship to something, often what is possessed: I possess my car, my home, and so on. In the case of the gift of the Holy Spirit as a *genitive of identity*: it draws our attentions to what we have received with the divine indwelling—the very identity of God.

Pray in the Spirit

Tip 1: Invite the Holy Spirit into Your Life

My wife and I would often have passing conversations with couples at Mass, but that was it, just passing conversations. It was not until we started to invite these couples over for dinner that we really got to know them. We invited, and they responded; we opened the door (both to our home and to our hearts), and they entered. We now speak with them regularly, no longer in brief interactions after Mass, but in substantial conversations—conversations that are full of meaning, life-giving, fruitful.

Our goal should be to have the best possible life-giving conversation—one with the Holy Spirit. For the Holy Spirit is the life-giving communication between the Father and the Son that brings the fullness of meaning into every conversation and situation.

Inviting the presence of the Holy Spirit into our prayer is the first tip of this book, because without it, our prayer would lack the necessary life-giving force to be what it ought to be. What the switch is to a light, the Holy Spirit is to our prayer.

To *invite* is to invoke, summon, call upon, or make an appeal. In our intercessory prayer, we are invoking the presence of God into our lives and making an appeal before Him to transform the life or situation for which we are praying. Jesus said He will be with us always (see Matt. 28:20), and by virtue of the gift of the Holy Spirit, He *is*!

Our invocation is the fruit of an interior action—the opening of our hearts. To invite the Holy Spirit into our lives of prayer is a response to an action that God has already performed. God is always one step ahead of us; He has first knocked on the doors of our hearts (see Rev. 3:20). Therefore, our first step toward Him is always a response to His initial invitation (see CCC 2567).

Jesus said, "Ask, and it will be given you; seek, and you will find; knock, and it will be opened to you" (Matt. 7:7). Behind every good asking, seeking, and knocking is the goodness of the

Holy Spirit. When talking about the Holy Spirit moving in our lives, it is not uncommon to use such words as "nudging," "prompting," and "motivating." All these words have their reference point in the Holy Spirit, who inspires. We are nudged, prompted, and motivated to do what we ought to do because we first have been inspired by the protagonist of all good prayer—the Holy Spirit. In intercessory prayer, we have so much more power than we realize, not power from within, but from without—the power of the Holy Spirit given to us as gift. When we pray without the Holy Spirit, we are without the breath of God (out of breath); when we pray in the Holy Spirit, we are full of breath—full of life!

The gift of the Holy Spirit is unlimited. In Christ's words, "For he whom God has sent utters the words of God, for it is not by measure that he gives the Spirit; the Father loves the Son and has given all things into his hand" (John 3:34–35). To paraphrase Father David Pivonka, President of Franciscan University of Steubenville, God does not portion out "a serving" of the Holy Spirit to each of us; instead, He gives all of the Holy Spirit to everyone—unmeasured.[7] As a people, we are not satisfied until we are full. We always want more. We want everything supersized. God is that "more" because He is infinite. He is the "supersize" because there is nothing superior to Him. The word "super" is derived from the Latin *supra*, meaning "above," and there is nothing above God.

As we invite the Holy Spirit into our prayer, we are inviting what is infinite in value. I have prayed for others while lacking confidence (faith) in what God would do for the one for whom I was praying. But to pray in the Spirit, who is the unmeasured gift, is to pray with confidence that God withholds nothing in our requests

---

[7]   Dave Pivonka, "God's Love Poured Out," segment 1, 22:59 (2016), Ministry of the Wild Goose, https://thewildgooseisloose.com/series-segments.

(see John 3:21–22). Even if God's response is not to our initial lik-ing, it remains infinite in its value because God's response always has salvation in mind. The deeper we go in our union with God, the more we understand His answers. Understanding follows trust.

One way to get at what this Holy Spirit–filled prayer looks like is to imitate the Spirit-filled prayer of Jesus.

Tip 2: Imitate the Spirit-filled Prayer of Jesus

We imitate what we hold in high regard. Growing up playing basket-ball, I imitated everything Michael Jordan did. I mean everything, from the finest detail of how he dribbled the ball up the court to the way in which he wore his socks. (Yes, I folded the top end of my socks as Jordan did.) In my mind, imitating everything Michael Jordan did was going to somehow make me a better basketball player.

In the spiritual life, we have the perfect reference point in Christ. Saint Paul said, "Be imitators of me, as I am of Christ" (1 Cor. 11:1). We imitate Saint Paul as he imitated Christ, and we imitate Christ because it will make us the best possible Christians we could be.[8]

In order to understand the Spirit-filled prayer of Jesus as the basis for our intercessory prayer, let's focus on the action of Jesus when He healed the deaf man with a speech impediment. "He put his fingers into his ears, and he spat and touched his tongue; and looking up to heaven, he sighed, and said to him, 'Ephphatha,' that is, 'Be opened'" (Mark 7:33–34). Note the initial action taken by Jesus: He "looked up." He looked up because power does not come from below but from above. So, too, intercessory prayer does not begin with a glance downward or ahead of us but with a glance upward. In fact, we pray on bended knee because it encourages the posture of looking up.

---

[8] To talk about this imitation would take a whole book (see *Imitation of Christ* by Thomas à Kempis).

Unleashing the Power of Intercessory Prayer

Jesus then "sighed deeply." Before He even uttered a word, He expressed a groan. Jesus sighs and groans because the best prayer always "digs deep." Often, when we push ourselves athletically, in the weight room or on the soccer field, we "dig deep" with sighs and groans. The God-Man encourages us to begin our prayers of intercession by "digging deep"—reaching into the innermost place of our faith in God with sighs and groans.

After Jesus looked up and sighed deeply, He uttered one word: *Ephphatha!* The Lord's command, "Be opened," performs a dual action. On the one hand, He commands the opening of the ears and loosening of the tongue of the deaf man so that he may be healed (see Mark 7:35). On the other hand, Jesus simultaneously commands that the heavens "be opened" so that the power and workings of God may be made manifest. We do not look up just to see the color of the sky or the birds flying by. We look up to see what lies beyond—the heavens. As we pray, we might envision heaven "opening up" on behalf of the one for whom we are praying.

As we pray on bended knee, we do so mindful that we are called to pray into the messiness of others. When Jesus "put his fingers" into the deaf man's ears and "spat and touched his tongue," He teaches us that Spirit-led prayer is not always pleasant. It can be downright bothersome, if not awkward. We should not have to be asked to pray for the homeless, the imprisoned, or whomever we deem "bothersome." God's invitation to share in His redemptive love should always include those on the margins of society. We pray for people not because of *who they are* but *because they are.* We have the power to pray for people into being, into a becoming, who they ought to be. There is a gap between the persons we are and the persons we ought to be, and our intercessory prayer is stepping into that gap and assisting others in their becoming.

A close reading of the Gospel of Mark suggests one more way in which we should imitate Christ in our intercessory prayer:

commentators have noted that whenever Jesus speaks in Aramaic in the Gospels, in every case, He prays with intimacy. Before Jesus restores Jairus's twelve-year-old daughter to life (see Mark 5:35–43), He dismisses all present except for the parents. As Jesus prays over the little girl, He employs the Aramaic *Talitha koum* ("Little girl, I say to you, 'Get up'"). This healing was personal. During the Passion, Jesus speaks the Aramaic *Abba* and *Eloi, Eloi, lema sabachthani?* These are cries of an intimate conversation—*Abba*, "Father," a cry of filial intimacy, and *Eloi, Eloi, lema sabachthani*, "My God, my God, why have you abandoned me," a question that rises from the intimacy of Christ's heart. Our Lord's praying in the Spirit was a prayer of closeness—this is why Saint Paul teaches that all good prayer begins with the cry, "Abba, Father!" (Rom. 8:15).

As we learn the language of looking up, sighing, and groaning—uttering words that call upon God to "open up" heaven—we learn the way of intimacy by imitating the prayer of Jesus. Indeed, "intercession is the prayer of petition which leads us to pray as Jesus did" (CCC 2634). To further deepen our Christlike prayer, we must learn to imitate His humility.

Tip 3: Walk Humbly in the Presence of the Holy Spirit

I love to go for walks. When I go for a walk with my wife, or my children, or my closest friends, they have my full attention. Whether in the park or on a hike, going for walks typically provides time for reflective conversation, which, in turn, enhances relationships. Personally, a stroll alongside our nearby lake inspires my most reflective conversations. And sometimes that conversation is with God.

Some of my best intercessory prayers have occurred when I went for a walk to be alone with God. God likes to go for walks and join you for yours: God walked in the garden in the cool of the day (see Gen. 3:8). The great patriarchs walked with God: Enoch (see Gen.

5:24), Noah (see Gen. 6:9), Abraham and Isaac (see Gen. 48:15). It is good to walk with God, and we do so by invoking the presence of the Holy Spirit and intentionally making Him a part of our every move (see Gal. 5:16; Rom. 8:4). This is a book concerning the *spiritual* life, and there is no *spiritual* life without a *life* in the Holy *Spirit*. Remember, prayer is personal, relational. Invite the Holy Spirit into all that you do, even your walks. Walk with the Holy Spirit!

The prophet Micah adds an essential dimension to this walk: "He has showed you, O man, what is good ... to walk *humbly* with your God" (Mic. 6:8, emphasis added). To walk in the presence of the Holy Spirit is to walk in the virtue of humility. Why? The Holy Spirit is the eternal exchange of love shared between the Father and the Son. This other-centered love is the necessary ingredient in the virtue of humility. The humble soul understands that he is no more or less important than his neighbor, so he never places himself first in the company of the other. The humble soul is never preoccupied with a bloated reputation, being "right" in a conversation, or having all the answers to all the world's problems. The humble soul is most free to love because this person never gets lost in the lies required to protect the false self. The humble soul does one thing: wills the good of others. It is this virtue of humility that is the fountainhead of all good intercessory prayer (see CCC 2559).

In the prayer of intercession, the humble soul who wills the good of others always looks to their interests, "even to the point of praying for those who do him harm" (CCC 2635). Maybe the person who hurt you did not ask, "Will you pray for me?" but, if someone has harmed you, then the person *needs* your prayer.

> But I say to you, *love your enemies and pray for those who persecute you, so that you may be sons of your Father in heaven....* For if you love those who love you, what reward have you? Do not even the tax collectors do the same? And if you salute only your

brethren, what more are you doing than others? Do not even the Gentiles do the same? You, therefore, must be perfect as your heavenly Father is perfect. (Matt. 5:44–48, emphasis added)

This is an extraordinary exhortation and a challenging truth! To be a Christian, we must do as Christ does, which means loving our neighbor *and* praying for those who oppress us. Here, I encourage you to ponder who that person is in your life and commit to praying for him or her. By virtue of God's grace, you can do it! Walk in the presence of the Holy Spirit and dedicate at least one prayer a day to praying for your enemy. Over time, this will turn into joy — the joy of being free from the bondage of anger and contempt.

Now, if you feel it is *unreasonable* to pray for the person who has persecuted you, remember the *reason* behind the Cross: atonement for sin. Unite your prayer with the heart of Christ on the Cross, and what initially appeared to be *unreasonable* prayer has its *reason*: the salvation of souls, including your own soul (see Phil. 2:12) and the soul of the person who is persecuting you. This, no doubt, calls for an interior revolution that is brought about by the virtue of humility.

As it is, we must will the good of others, including our enemies, by praying for them. This is no small order. Christ puts this challenge before us in the call to "be perfect as our heavenly Father is perfect (Matt. 5:48)." Begin by praying for your enemies in the Spirit, and do so with a "sigh" or a "groan" so that we might "pray as we ought" (Rom. 8:26). Pray in the Spirit!

Key Patron: Saint Maximilian Kolbe

As I prayed for insight into which saint ought to be our key patron for praying in the Spirit, I was led to Saint Maximilian Kolbe. This Franciscan is widely known for his missionary movement, the Militia Immaculata, and his heroic martyrdom in Auschwitz. He was also undoubtedly a man of and for the Holy Spirit. Through

his devotion to the Blessed Mother, Saint Maximilian Kolbe discovered a key insight into the life and prayer of the Holy Spirit.

But first, a word about his life.

Raymond Kolbe was born in 1894, and his experiences as a child
were like those of most children, with one dramatic exception.
One night, after his mother expressed concern about what was to
become of young Raymond, he prayed to Mary. It was then that
Mary appeared to him with two crowns: one red and one white. In
the words of Saint Maximilian Kolbe, "She asked if I was willing to
accept either of these crowns. The white one meant that I should
persevere in purity and the red that I should become a martyr. I said
that I would accept them both."[9] Indeed, he accepted them both; he
was ordained to the priesthood at the age of twenty-four and died a
martyr seventeen years later in a starvation bunker in Auschwitz.[10]

Among the many great achievements[11] of Saint Maximilian's
life was the establishment of the largest formation house in all of
Europe with an evangelization center in the city of Niepokalanow,
which means "the city of the Immaculata." From 1927 to 1939, the
formation house expanded from eighteen friars to nine hundred.
Saint Maximilian also established a seminary in Nagasaki, Japan.
Because he decided not to build his seminary on the "propitious"
side of the mountain, it survived the blast of the atomic bomb in

[9] "Kolbe, Saint of Auschwitz," The Holocaust, http://www.auschwitz.
dk/kolbe.htm.

[10] For this action, Pope John Paul II declared him the patron saint
of our difficult age. The man he gave his life for in Auschwitz,
Franciszek Gajowniczek, devoted many years to letting the world
know what Maximilian Kolbe did for him. He was also there for
Maximilian's canonization.

[11] He had a genius-level intellect and was an astrophysicist. His
intense interest in space flight led him to design a "shuttle-like"
aircraft. He sought to patent it, but World War II and his calling
to the Militia Immaculata closed that door.

1945. Saint Maximilian was a man inspired by the Holy Spirit to do great things for the Kingdom of God.

And with that, I put before us Saint Maximilian Kolbe as our patron for this opening key: praying in the Spirit.

Saint Maximilian Kolbe's devotion to the Holy Spirit was the fruit of his devotion to the Blessed Virgin Mary. His reflections upon the Holy Spirit are, without exception, the consequence of his meditation upon Mary. We see this explicitly in his reflection upon the Holy Spirit as the uncreated Immaculate Conception.

In 1858, just four years after Mary was defined dogmatically as the Immaculate Conception,[12] Mary appeared to Bernadette Soubirous in the small town of Lourdes, France. When Bernadette asked the "lady" her name, Mary responded, "I am the Immaculate Conception." For Saint Maximilian Kolbe, Mary, the *created* Immaculate Conception, led him to a reflection upon the Holy Spirit as the *uncreated* Immaculate Conception.

What is meant by this phrase, *uncreated* Immaculate Conception? God is the uncreated, infinite existence of immaculate love. The Holy Spirit is the immaculate love shared between the Father and the Son. Thus, as uncreated God and as the love between the Father and the Son, the Holy Spirit is the uncreated conception of immaculate love. For Saint Maximilian Kolbe, "the Holy Spirit is an uncreated conception, an eternal one; he is the prototype of every sort of human conception ... infinitely holy, Immaculate."[13]

---

[12] In the dogma of the Immaculate Conception, defined in 1854, the Church proclaimed that Mary, from the first moment of her conception, was freed from the stain of Original Sin. In other words, Mary, full of grace (see Luke 1:28), was freed from the sinful inclinations that have plagued man since the time of the Fall.

[13] Fr. H. M. Manteau-Bonamy, O.P., *Immaculate Conception and the Holy Spirit: The Marian Teachings of Saint Maximilian Kolbe* (Marytown, IL: Marytown Press, 2008), 57.

Unleashing the Power of Intercessory Prayer

We cannot underestimate the value of what Saint Maximilian is saying here. In particular, "the Holy Spirit ... is the prototype of every sort of human conception." If we desire our prayers to bring about something new and beautiful—something *holy conceived* from the infinite mind of God—for the person or situation for which we are praying—then we need to fervently invoke the Holy Spirit for those people and situations. When the Holy Spirit acts, He is always and everywhere saying: "Behold, I make all things new" (Rev. 21:5). If the Holy Spirit is love, and love is action of willing good, then the Holy Spirit is the action, par excellence, that transforms all things into something new, beautiful, and good.

When it comes to prayer in the Spirit, Saint Maximilian Kolbe offers us an example not only to behold but to emulate. From his studies in Rome, when he launched a renewal of Marian devotion, to Auschwitz, when he surrendered his life for a prisoner he did not know, Father Maximilian Kolbe was untiringly inviting the presence of the Holy Spirit into his life in order to will the good of others. He was deeply intimate with God and courageously walked the path of humility. He lived up to his name—he was in one word, "great!"[14]

Saint Maximilian Kolbe, pray for us!

Prompt Questions for Journaling

1. Do you have a personal relationship with the Holy Spirit? Do you have *passing* conversations or *substantial* conversations with Him?
2. What are the ways you can increase in humility in your walk with God?

---

[14] The name Maximillian is derived from the Latin *Maximus*, which translates as "greatest."

2

Pray in Faith

I have hailed Roger Federer's tennis achievements as "unbelievable." I have deemed the instrumental skills of the Piano Guys "unbelievable." I used the same adjective after watching daredevil Nik Wallenda walk a tightrope across the gorge of the Grand Canyon.

In these cases, "unbelievable" describes excellence (Federer), astonishing skill (Piano Guys), and something so bold that it borders on the extreme (Wallenda). In some, if not all, cases, what is excellent, astonishing, extreme—what is unbelievable—seems too astounding or too enjoyable to be true. My wedding day was "unbelievable" in this sense; it was excellent, astonishing, intensely exciting, and seemingly too enjoyable to be true.

Why is it that we so often make the term "unbelievable" synonymous with "too good to be true"? I suggest it has something to do with how we instinctually claim heaven to be unbelievable. The promise of heaven is so excellent, so astonishing, and so intensely exciting that it is almost impossible to believe, so we say "unbelievable." Yet describing heaven as "unbelievable" has a different meaning from describing the actions of others as "unbelievable." Our recognition of another's feat has little or no bearing on our salvation. Our *faith in God* as Creator and Father of all that is excellent, astonishing, and intensely exciting lies at the heart of our salvation.

Unleashing the Power of Intercessory Prayer

Faith claims: "I believe in the unbelievable." When we take this kind of faith into our prayer, the fruit in our lives leaves those around us saying, "This is too good to be true," and yet faith claims it is true!

Intercessory Key: Pray in Faith

Faith is primary because it is a theological virtue, meaning that it comes directly from God. Through His grace, the doors to our hearts are opened to Him. Whenever we approach God in faith, we ought to have confidence in Christ's words that "all things are possible to him who believes" (Mark 9:23). The Letter to the Hebrews reminds us, "Without faith it is impossible to please him. For whoever would draw near to God must believe that he exists and that he rewards those who seek him" (Heb. 11:6). By praying in faith, we draw near to God, and all good intercessory prayer is a drawing near to God.

First, faith is a gift received (see Eph. 2:8–9) — a gift infused into our souls at Baptism. As a gift, it is not something we "purchase" or even merit; instead, it is something we receive out of God's sheer lavishness.

Second, faith is an act — the act of confidently listening and responding to God. First and foremost, faith is a response to God, who is love. Out of our commitment to God, our faith in Him, and our love for Him, we act in a way that follows His laws. So, as we set out on the path of intercessory prayer, we set out in faith, acting in a way that shows our love for and *faith*fulness to God. It does us immeasurable good to make our first step on this path a prayer for an increase of faith.

Tip 1: Pray for an Increase in Faith

Tips are aids for improvement. We have tips for everything: tips to increase your energy level, to live longer, to make more friends, to better intercede for others in prayer. Tips can help us to expand upon what we already have and already know, including matters in the spiritual life.

Do we pray for an increase in faith? God desires that we do so. In the Gospel of Mark, Jesus encounters a boy who is possessed by a demon (see Mark 9:14–29). When Jesus asks how long the boy has been possessed, the father responds, "From childhood.... *If you can* do anything, have pity on us and help us" (Mark 9:21–22). Our Lord responds, "'*If you can!*' All things are possible to him who believes" (Mark 9:23). In contemporary terminology, Jesus could well have said, "Really? Did you just ask me if I can? The problem is not with me and what I can do, but with you and your lack of faith!" The phrase "If you can" implies doubt. Evidently, the message got through to the boy's father, who "cried out" with my favorite prayer in Scripture (excluding the Our Father), "I believe, help my unbelief" (Mark 9:24). In this crying out to God, the boy's father prays for an increase in faith. Let us not pray first, "God, if you can," but, "Lord, I believe, help my unbelief."[15]

Prayer in faith points to a deep reality — that faith is a gift received only from God. In principle, a gift must come from someone outside the self. The "I" can never give himself a gift — the very nature of a gift must always include the other. In our Christmas gift exchanges, if we pull our own name out of the hat, we put it back. Why? Because we instinctually know that in gift-giving "I" needs "other." In relationship to faith, the "other" is "Thou" — God! Let us make this our prayer, "I believe, help my unbelief."

God is inexhaustible; He is the "always more" and therefore can give endlessly. As we go on bended knee to pray for others,

---

[15] Bear in mind, the person in Scripture who is synonymous with doubt, Thomas, robustly prayed: "My Lord and my God!" (John 20:28). This is a great prayer of faith!

let us always ask for more faith! And as we do, let us pray with the confidence that God is listening to our spirit-filled prayers.

Tip 2: Pray with Confidence

We have all heard the platitude "practice makes perfect." Like all platitudes, this phrase is trite and lacks evidential support, but it hints at truth. In the case of "practice makes perfect," practice will never bring perfection, but it will maximize our potential in the given area of pursuit. Sometimes a person can achieve excellence. But the truth behind "practice makes perfect" is less about excellence and more about what practice builds — confidence. Talk with an athlete or a musician; he or she will not equate practice with excellence but with confidence. Coaches will spend more time building up a player than praising his excellence (although praise can be a form of building up). In everything we do, confidence precedes excellence and distinction. Repetition then builds confidence, and confidence leads to belief.

What is true in sports and music is infinitely truer in the call to pray with confidence. Just as the athlete who trains devotedly sees his talents grow, so, too, the one who prays will see his relationship with God grow.

Prayer is conversation with God, and as already highlighted, conversation serves the fundamental purpose of getting to know another. What happens when we get to know others? We trust others more. When we pray with confidence, we learn the language of trust. In fact, the Latin root for confidence is *fidere*, "to trust." The more we talk with God, the more confidence we will have in Him. Here, we ought to be reminded of the ancient principle that undergirds all truth: what you feed grows. The more time you spend with something, the more you will be attached to it. Vice begets vice; virtue begets virtue. Necessarily, prayer leads to trust in God, and trust leads to a greater conviction in prayer, including in our intercessions.

Holding up our petitions of intercession with confidence is the great act of faith and the real conviction that God feels our every ache and hears our every word. Trust says, "I believe." Trust says, "Amen."

Such was the conviction of the Roman centurion whose story appears in Matthew 8. After Jesus told him that He would go to his home to heal his paralyzed servant, the centurion responded, "Lord, I am not worthy to have you come under my roof; but only say the word, and my servant will be healed. . . . When Jesus heard him, he marveled, and said to those who followed him, 'Truly, I say to you, not even in Israel have I found such faith'" (Matt. 8:8–10). The spiritual confidence of the Roman centurion teaches us that trust is the most concrete act of faith,[16] invaluable to our prayer of intercession. Because the centurion went to Jesus in faith, his servant was healed. Note, at the end of the narrative, Jesus does not say: "Go, I have made him well." Or, more simply, "Go, he is well." Instead, Jesus says, "Go, be it done for you as you have believed." It is apparent that Jesus wants us to know that the centurion's faith was essential to the healing—this cannot be underestimated! In our petitions of intercession, we would be well served to echo the trust-filled words of the centurion, "But only say the word, and [my prayer will be answered]."

---

[16] Incidentally, the inclusion of the prayer of the Roman centurion into the prayer we pray right before receiving the Eucharist is a beautiful reminder that our intercessory prayers during Mass are to be offered in a humble love filled with confidence. Note the slight change from the words of the centurion in what we pray during Mass. The centurion says, "Lord, I am not worthy to have you come under my roof; but only say the word, and my servant shall be healed" (Matt. 8:8). We utter the same words but replace "my servant shall be healed" with "my soul shall be healed." We are made to see that we are the servants who need healing.

Unleashing the Power of Intercessory Prayer

As confidence is synonymous with trust, so trust is synonymous with faith. The Greek word for "faith," *pistis*, which can be found 243 times in the New Testament, best translates as "trust." Throughout the Old and New Testaments, the actions of faith that were praised were effects of trust.

Note that trust is a reasonable and expected human experience. We do it every day in the ordinary course of life. When you get on a plane, get into a taxicab, or take a prescription, you are trusting that the pilot, taxicab driver, and doctor are all licensed to perform their professional duties and will perform them well. God is eminently worthy of trust, and so we ought to trust Him with everything. Read the lives of the saints and be inspired to trust more. At times, saints lacked trust, but they prayed: "I trust; help my lack of trust."

As we intercede on behalf of others, we need to stand firm in trust because, again, God does not always respond to our intercessory petitions with a "yes" but sometimes with a "no" or "not yet." In God, there is no indecisiveness—even His "not yet" is what is decisive to His infinite plan. Turning this idea inside out, we could assert that God always says "yes" to what is suitable for our salvation, but we hear it as a "no" or "not yet" because we do not always understand God's infinite design for the salvation of souls. For many of us, myself included, we would love a Post-it note from God explaining the meaning of our (supposedly) unanswered prayers. Instead, He asks us to trust in His word and to persevere with a steadfast heart (see James 1:4). With a steadfast heart, we learn the language of the perfect prayer: "Thy will be done."

Not every good is a good willed by God. No matter how God responds to our intercessory petitions, we should never be detracted from entrusting our prayers to Him. Our intercessions should continually open us up to the Father's loving plan of salvation for all people (this will be revisited in chapter 6). As we abandon ourselves

26

to God's infinite design, we do so mindful that the Spirit adds His voice to our sometimes-wordless moans, making whole our prayer of petition before God the Father.

In the Old Testament, we have the shining example of our "father in faith," Abraham (Rom. 4:16). Why is Abraham our father in faith? Because "by faith [*pistis*] Abraham, when he was tested, offered up Isaac" (Heb. 11:17). Just as Abraham's offering was an offering of trust, so, too, must our prayers of intercession be offerings of "trust."

Tip 3: Heed the Lesson from Our Father in Faith

We normally seek advice from those who are seasoned or credentialed, or both, in the area in which we wish to grow. If I do not know my way around a W-2 or a Form 1120 at tax time, it is best to seek the advice of a tax accountant. We turn to experts because they have something important to teach us. As we seek to be more coherent in our praying in faith, it would behoove us to receive guidance from an expert, our "father in faith," Abraham.

The narrative of Abraham takes up fourteen chapters in the book of Genesis (see Gen. 12–25), and at the center of its developing plot is a story that the Hebrews call the *Akedah*, "the binding of Isaac." At first glance, the whole of this narrative seems to put God in contradiction with Himself.

The Abrahamic narrative begins with a divine call: "Now the Lord said to Abram 'Go from your country and your kindred and your country's house to the land that I will show you'" (Gen. 12:1). Promises of great blessing accompany this exhortation: "And I will make of you a great nation, and I will bless you, and make your name great, so that you will be a blessing. I will bless those who bless you, and him who curses you I will curse; and by you all the families of the earth shall bless themselves" (Gen. 12:2–3). Years pass, and at a very elderly age, Abraham's wife, Sarah, bears a son, Isaac. Isaac is everything to Abraham—his beloved son and the one through whom his line will prevail, through whom he will indeed become the father to many nations.

Fast-forward twelve more years, and what does God ask Abraham to do? Sacrifice his son as an offering to Him. "After these things God tested Abraham, and said to him, 'Abraham!' And he said, 'Here am I.' He said, 'Take your son, your only son Isaac, whom you love, and go to the land of Moriah, and offer him there as a burnt offering upon one of the mountains of which I shall tell you" (Gen. 22:1–2). Imagine, the same God that promised him the title "father of many nations" now asked Abraham to kill his son.

Typically, God's request of Abraham confounds the reader on two levels. First, God is love. How could a God of love ask us to murder someone? And what loving father asks another father to kill his son? Second, if Abraham kills his son, he then kills his line, which was to be blessed with "many nations." For many of us, we read this story and scratch our heads. Here, the God of the Bible appears to be the God of inconsistency. Into this apparent contradiction, Abraham's faith speaks to us.

On the level of reason, it is fair to ask, "What may have been going through the mind of Abraham when he was asked to offer his own son as a holocaust to God?" Possibly, it had something to do with love.

God is absolute Love (see 1 John 4:16). As already noted, love is the virtue that wills the good of others for the sake of others, expecting nothing in return. Love, by its very nature, possesses no self-interestedness. This is the essence of God: absolute unselfishness. As my professor from Oxford once said, "God wills our best interest because there is no selfishness in God." On the level of reason, I believe Abraham's conviction was that he was not obedient to an oppressor, but obedient to a God who only wanted the best for him. Reason alone cannot explain Abraham's heroic faith in obeying this most puzzling request to murder his son. Reason alone could never explain Abraham's response. Because of this, his response of faith, he is our "father of faith"—his most significant conviction was to believe what he did not see (see Heb. 11:1; John 20:29).

Abraham's lesson is this: remember *Who* it is that asks so much from us. Our God is a God who has not an iota of self-interestedness in Him. God loves us more than we could ever hope to love ourselves. We are not slaves in a master-slave relationship, but children in a loving father-child relationship. Fathers ask their children to trust them because fathers know *better*. God the Father asks for radical trust because God the Father knows what's *best*!

The lesson of Abraham's faith does not end there. To read carefully the fourteen chapters that depict the story of Abraham is also to become aware of his lack of trust and art of deception. To protect himself, on two separate occasions, Abraham claims Sarah as his sister: first to the pharaoh (see Gen. 12:10–20) and second to King Abimelech (see Gen. 20:1–5). In the case of his encounter with the pharaoh, he pretends to be Sarah's brother, and the pharaoh eventually takes Sarah as his wife (see Gen. 12:10–20). Abraham probably did not expect his deception to end with Sarah going into the pharaoh's house, but deception always has consequences.

What is the additional lesson here? Great faith can arise from considerable doubt. We tend to be scrupulous of our doubt and become entrapped by our lack of faith. God wants us to remember that He believes in us, despite our lack of confidence. Here again lies the importance of praying for an increase in faith.

In the end, over time, Abraham cultivated his faith in God, and as he did, he learned to trust in God's ways. "Not knowing where he was to go" (Heb. 11:8), he confidently listened to God. I hope that our prayer in faith is filled with a confident listening that will make us better intercessors of prayer. Pray in faith!

Key Patron: Saint Gianna Beretta Molla

When I first learned of Saint Gianna Beretta Molla, I was surprised by her story. She is not a saint who had mystical visions of Jesus, a Doctor of the Church who gave us some insightful treatise, or a figure who started a religious community. Saint Gianna was a wife, a mother, and a physician who appeared to live an ordinary life.

At first glance, the details of Saint Gianna's life were rather usual. Her enjoyment of skiing and mountain climbing were not uncommon to the inhabitants of Bergamo, the region of Italy from which she hailed. Her involvements in the Saint Vincent de Paul Society and the Catholic Action Movement, while noble, are not the supernatural details that typically emerge when reading about saints. She was a loving wife and mother who practiced medicine, came from a family of thirteen, and had four children of her own. When reading about her for the first time, I still remember thinking, "Saint Gianna's life is not so different from mine! I come from a family of eleven and have four children. My wife mothers them with great love, and she practices medicine, too." It was after working through these initial details, however, that I encountered what made her a saintly woman. It was not so much what she did, as it was the love and the faith that she put into it.

The deeper I dug, the more evidence I found of the great love and deep faith that sanctified her everyday life. Saint Gianna's time in the mountains was an opportunity to be close to God. If creation is God's first love letter to man, then skiing and mountain climbing were her ways of faithfully engaging with this love letter. The mountains were a place she could go to be "in tune" with God. Her involvement with the Saint Vincent de Paul Society and the

Catholic Action Movement was not to console her conscience but a response of great love and faith to serve those on the margins and meet Christ in the poor. There, she would put her profession of medicine to great use. Every day she accepted God's will, and she responded to His calls in great confidence by becoming a wife, mother, and physician.

In 1961, Gianna's confidence in God was tested when, while in the first trimester of her fourth pregnancy, she experienced great abdominal pain. After a series of procedures, doctors discovered that she had developed a fibroma in her uterus—she was carrying a baby and a tumor.

There were three options before Gianna Molla: have a hysterectomy; have an abortion, which would kill the baby but save her life and allow her to have more children; or have the tumor removed, which would put her life at risk, but save the baby's. Heroically, against the doctor's counsel, Gianna placed her baby's life before her own. She had the tumor removed without the hysterectomy, and in April of 1962, Gianna Emanuela Molla was born.[17] As anticipated, a week after the birth of little Gianna, the elder Gianna died due to postoperative complications.

In our third tip, I emphasized following in the footsteps of our spiritual forefather, Abraham, and his great obedience of faith. Gianna Molla walked that same path profoundly. In the *Akedah*—the binding of Isaac—God asked Abraham to offer his son to Him, and with great faithfulness, he did precisely that. In the case of Gianna Molla, God asked her to offer herself on behalf of her daughter, and she did precisely that.

Occasionally in our life experiences, someone comes along and reminds us that what we do every day—what is perceived to be ordinary—is an opportunity for God to transform the usual into

---

[17] Emanuela means "God is with us."

unusual. Holiness is the "holy unusual" way of God. Saint Gianna embraced the "holy unusual" way of God and is a shining example of trusting in Him.

Saint Gianna Beretta Molla, pray for us!

Prompt Questions for Journaling

1. Do you pray for an increase of faith? If so, how has this changed your prayer for others? If not, begin the practice of doing so and reflect on the impact it has in your intercessory prayer.

2. In what areas of your life have you repeatedly practiced something to find it bearing fruit? Reflect upon this and its influence on your intercessory prayer.

3

Pray from the Heart

In my early twenties, I became fascinated with studies on the human embryo. While attending college, I audited a course on embryology. What I learned in that class could fill many pages in this book, but there was one truth that stood out among many: the primacy and vitality of the heart.

The human heart is the first functional organ to develop. It begins beating and pumping blood around day twenty-one or twenty-two. So, before most women even know they are pregnant, their babies' hearts beat. Among other things, "this emphasizes the critical nature of the heart in the distribution of blood through the vessels and the vital exchange of nutrients, oxygen, and wastes both to and from the developing baby." These critical functions are reflected in the prominent heart bulge that appears in the sonogram.[18]

As the baby grows, so does the heart, continuing to show itself as the most vital organ in the body. The heart beats more than 100,000 times per day and 35 million times per year, which equates to more than 2.5 billion times in one life span. Simply put, the heart is the primordial and vital life source of the functioning of our bodies.

---

[18] See "Development of the Heart," *Anatomy and Physiology*, chap. 19, OpenStax, https://openstax.org/books/anatomy-and-physiology/pages/19-5-development-of-the-heart.

Unleashing the Power of Intercessory Prayer

As is often the case, what is true in the physical world is also true in the spiritual world: the heart matters.

Intercessory Key: Pray from the Heart

To pray from the heart is to pray from the most interior place of your being—the place where the Holy Spirit dwells. In the words of the *Catechism of the Catholic Church*:

> The heart is the dwelling-place where I am, where I live; according to the Semitic or Biblical expression, the heart is the place "to which I withdraw." The heart is our hidden center, beyond the grasp of our reason and of others; only the Spirit of God can fathom the human heart and know it fully. The heart is the place of decision, deeper than our psychic drives. It is the place of truth, where we choose life or death. It is the place of encounter, because as image of God we live in relation: it is the place of covenant. (2563)

The Hebrew and Greek words for the "heart" can be found more than one thousand times in Sacred Scripture, making it the most anthropological term used in the Bible. The heart is the center of who we are, and everything we do flows to and from it (see Prov. 4:23).

Praying from the heart is imperative to effective intercessory prayer. The Holy Spirit enlivens our prayer, yet when we invite Him into our lives, He needs a place to live. The heart is exactly the place for Him to do so. Increased prayer transforms our hearts into mansions—spaces big enough to hold and keep the Holy Spirit. After the death of St. Philip Neri, his heart was found to be enlarged, not because of disease, but because he prayed and loved greatly. His heart was physically inflamed by the Holy Spirit.

When we pray from the heart, we seek and find (see Jer. 29:13).

Tip 1: From Their Heart, to Your Heart, to His Heart

As a professor in spiritual theology, I often engage in matters of the heart. On one occasion, I was reflecting on the relationship between salvation and the call to become vulnerable. After the lecture and discussion, I received a very short message in my inbox with the title "Most difficult" and the text "becoming vulnerable." While this was a point I talked about in class, I found this message poignant. I stared at the screen, reflecting upon its deep truth: becoming vulnerable is most difficult.

When praying from our hearts, it is important to remember that someone else has first shared his heart. For it is the heart of another that should be our preoccupation. On occasion, it is "most difficult" to ask someone to pray for us because we feel that it may expose our failings and shortcomings. Consequently, we choose not to go to our friend and ask, "Will you pray for me?"

Why is it so much easier to go to others on behalf of someone else? It is because asking for prayers for another does not require the vulnerability that asking for oneself requires. In the past, I have suffered in my spiritual life because I was too prideful to admit that I needed prayer. Over time, I realized that becoming vulnerable is the key that unlocks God's plan of salvation for me, and by God's grace, I am now willing (some of the time) to take my weakness to others and request intercessory prayer.

Here, great insight is gained by considering the deeper meaning of salvation and vulnerability. The word "salvation" is derived from the Latin word *salvare*, meaning "to save." It's root *salve*, translates as "balm," as in a healing balm that restores. The word "vulnerable" is derived from the Latin *vulnerare*—the root of which translates as "wound"—what one receives when being struck. During His Passion, our Lord made Himself vulnerable by being struck. He takes on our wounds by becoming the wounded, and as He does, He becomes the *healing balm* (salve) that restores us to the purity of our origins. The God-Man teaches us that salvation passes by way of addressing the wound, and if we wish to attain salvation, we do so in "fear and trembling" (Phil. 2:12) by becoming vulnerable. Salvation's pathway may very well be the most difficult, but it's worth it.

This truth also suggests that there is a connection between the vulnerability of Christ as Intercessor and the disposition one takes in intercessory prayer. It's not just the one asking for prayer who becomes vulnerable. The intercessor must take on some of the pain of the one he is praying for in order to pray *from the heart* (we will see this explicitly in our tip on fasting).

Take it to heart when people share with you their most "hidden centers," and then pray for them from the heart whole*heart*edly.

Tip 2: Pray Wholeheartedly

In many ways, the key to *praying from the heart* is my reason for writing this book. Far too often, my response, "Yes, I will pray for you," was half-hearted and distracted. All too much, I didn't follow through on my promise to do so. When we ask people to do something for us, we do not want them to go halfway but all the way. In school, 50 percent is an F (we have failed); 75 percent is a C (we are average); 85 percent is a B (we are above average). We shoot for the 100 percent because this is what it takes to achieve excellence. Everyone is more than just average; we are jewels of God's creation. Each soul deserves better-than-average prayer. If we want our prayers for others to be what they ought to be, then pray with 100 percent of your heart; pray wholeheartedly.

What is it that gets in the way of this wholehearted prayer? Among other things, impurity and distractions. In the Sermon on the Mount, Jesus says, "Blessed are the pure in heart, for they shall see God" (Matt. 5:8). The Greek word for "pure" is *katharos*, which translates as "pure," "clean," or "without mixture." In principle, the pure of heart are the single-hearted for God — those whose hearts are not ravaged by impurities. In its worst form, contamination of the heart includes the muck and mire of wrath, vengeance, pornography, and so on. In lesser things, this impurity is found in side glances and dwelling on unholy things. One overcomes this filth by way of repentance and intentional resolve to concentrate on the godly things: frequenting Confession and Mass, being present to those in need, hanging out with Christian friends with holy conversation, and watching only wholesome programs (to name a few). The many practices of holiness will keep our hearts focused on the holy One![19]

God's love refines our hearts (see Ps. 66:10; Prov. 17:3). As the silversmith uses fire to purge waste from metal, so God uses the fire of His love to cleanse away our iniquity. This cleansing takes place in the sacrament of Confession and the resolve to live out the corporal and spiritual works of mercy.[20] Give your whole heart

---

[19] This paragraph highlights the importance of repentance in the spiritual life. Repentance comes from the Greek term *metanoia*, which translates as a "change of mind." In Scripture, it represents a turning away from sin and turning toward God. When we repent, we experience a "change of mind" as our minds, bodies, and souls decidedly make the effort to avoid all occasions of sin and pursue God.

[20] The corporal works of mercy are acts of compassion where we assist our neighbors with their material and physical needs: give drink to the thirsty, feed the hungry, shelter the homeless, clothe the naked, visit the sick and the imprisoned, bury the dead, and give alms to the poor. The spiritual works of mercy, no less important than the corporal, are acts of compassion that help our neighbors in their emotional and spiritual needs: instruct the ignorant, counsel the doubtful, admonish the sinner, comfort the sorrowful, forgive offenses willingly, bear wrongs patiently, and pray for the living and the dead.

to God, and He will make it whole for you and for your brothers and sisters in Christ.

In my journey of faith, I realized that to offer wholehearted prayer to God, I needed to become more single-hearted (*katharos*) in my intentions, to overcome my half-heartedness. I was allowing the busyness of my days to drag me down. My heart had become a heart of stone. Our confidence when we pray in the Spirit is that we no longer have hearts of stone, but hearts of flesh (see Ezek. 36:26) — hearts that have been set on fire by the warmth and love of God. My heart had grown cold. I was failing to "see God" in the most important things in my life, for example, in praying for others. Be assured, as I continue to internalize the importance of being single-hearted for God, my intercessory prayer becomes warmer and more whole by the day.

The Bible has many examples of men and women who pray wholeheartedly. I am particularly fond of the exchange between Isaiah and King Hezekiah. In 2 Kings 20:1–3, the prophet Isaiah tells King Hezekiah he will die. In response to this message, King Hezekiah prays with tears: "Remember now, O Lord, I beseech thee, how I have walked before thee in faithfulness, and a whole heart, and done what is good in thy sight" (2 Kings 20:3). God responds to King Hezekiah, "I have heard your prayer, I have seen your tears" (2 Kings 20:5). God answers Hezekiah's unreserved, tear-filled, wholehearted prayer by adding fifteen years to his life.

God wants more than just lip service (see Isa. 29:13) or intention-less prayer; He wants a people who seek Him with their whole heart (see Ps. 119:2). What does Jesus say to the Pharisees? "This people honors me with their lips, but their heart is far from me" (Matt. 15:8). Prayer fails when it does not come from the heart. Jesus flunked the Pharisees on prayer. Half-hearted prayer fails; wholehearted prayer scores an A. I, for one, am humbled by the F grade, because again, there is a reason I am writing this book. Jesus wants us to mean what we say and say what we mean. If we say we are going to pray for someone, then pray for that someone wholeheartedly. Mean it! Remember, God sees the heart (see 1 Sam. 16:7).

In my struggle to pray wholeheartedly, as I examined my conscience, I discovered that I was giving my heart to lesser things —namely, material wants and desires. In giving my heart to lesser things, I was giving, at best, a D effort in my intercessory prayer. As difficult as it was to admit, I was like the rich young man (minus the rich), lacking the necessary wholehearted response for which Jesus was asking (see Matt. 19:16–30).

When the rich young man asks Jesus what he must do to inherit eternal life, Jesus calls him to follow the Ten Commandments. In response to this, the ambitious man says that he has always followed the commandments, so Jesus replies, "Go, sell what you possess, and give to the poor, and you will have treasure in heaven; and come, follow me" (Matt. 19:21). At this, the rich young man walked away sad because he treasured his possessions. I always thought this to be the most tragic of all episodes in the Gospel because it is the tragedy of half-heartedness. The rich young man's heart was tied to lesser things—he treasured material wealth over the spiritual wealth of Christ Himself. Let's be clear: the center of this tragedy is that he did not accept the invitation to receive God's mercy. The answer to the rich young man's question is not just a way of life, but *the* life—God! And the rich young man did not see God because of his attachment to worldly treasure.

So we must ask ourselves: What do we treasure? It's an important question. Jesus told us, "For where your treasure is, there will your heart be also" (Matt. 6:21). If our hearts are not in it, then our praying for others will go stale and stagnant. Pray with your whole heart, everything you have, and God will take care of the rest.

But what if your heart is broken and not whole? What if all you have to give is 50 percent? Let's be real; it is hard to pray with your whole heart when you are the one who is afflicted and suf-fering. In these cases, if all you have is 50 percent to give, or, for that matter, 1 percent to give, give 100 percent of the 50 percent you have, or 100 percent of the 1 percent you have. Maximize your efforts in whatever you have to give, and as you do, pray with Jesus on the Cross.

There is much to gain when we pray in the shadow of the Cross. On the Cross, Jesus takes everything that is broken, wounded, half of what it was and makes it whole again. Metaphorically speaking, the heart of Jesus was broken on the Cross, cut in half, yet from His "half"-hearted prayer came one of the most powerful prayers ever said: "Father, forgive them, for they know not what they do" (Luke 23:34). He prayed 100 percent into His brokenness. Among other things, Jesus wants to tell us: "If your heart is broken, that is okay; so was mine. I am with you, and this is how you pray — with everything you've got!"

In the case of praying with a broken heart, we may find ourselves in solidarity with the soul who has asked for our prayers. Often, when someone has asked for our prayers, they have done so out of brokenness. To pray for someone's brokenness out of our own brokenness is a powerful expression of solidarity and of the heart's merciful gaze upon the other's soul.[21] When suffering ministers to suffering, you have the most beautiful kind of mercy because it is the full bloom of love — love given, love received, and love shared (Trinitarian love)!

That being said, God desires to restore our brokenness. In this tip of praying wholeheartedly, we ought to be aware that the Lord's primary concern is to make our hearts whole. When the stretcher bearers brought the paralytic to Jesus, before Jesus physically healed

---

[21] "Mercy" is derived from the Latin *misericordia*, which roughly trans-lates as having a heart for those in misery.

him, He told him, "Take heart, my son, your sins are forgiven" (Matt. 9:2). In other words, Jesus says, "Before I restore your limbs as empirical evidence of my healing power, my first desire is to restore your heart. I heal from the inside out. Your sins are forgiven." When we serve as stretcher bearer for a good friend who has a physical malady and we "bring" that ailment to Jesus to heal, let us always remember God's preference for the heart because that's the place where He desires to abide.

Tip 3: Intercede as a Contemplative

Up to this point, we have placed an emphasis on the importance of making audible our prayers of intercession, which is certainly important. However, in contemplation we discover the most personal form of prayer as it embodies praying from the heart, where we encounter God in silence, submission, and love. In contemplation, we first gather up the heart and "recollect our whole being under the prompting of the Holy Spirit" (CCC 2711). This recollection situates us "in the dwelling place of the Lord which we are and awakens our faith in order to enter into the presence of him who awaits us" (CCC 2711). The recollected soul is then able to behold the One we know loves us, engaging in "the intense gaze of faith, fixed on Jesus" (CCC 2715).

Incidentally, the word "contemplation" is derived from the Latin *contemplatio*, which translates as "the act of looking at." The Latin root of the word "contemplation" is *templum*, which means "sacred." Pulling this together, and considering the above definition, we could say that contemplation is the act of looking at (intense gaze) that which is most sacred (Jesus). "'I look at him and he looks at me': this is what a certain peasant of Ars in the time of [Saint John Vianney] used to say while praying before the tabernacle" (CCC 2715).

Unleashing the Power of Intercessory Prayer

The "act of looking at" is a powerful expression of the love shared in contemplative prayer. Often, I find myself just "looking at" my wife. As the years pass, and I get to know her more, I find my *looking at her* to be more intense than it was when we first met — this is true both in our relationship and the contemplation of God. Just as my heart becomes absorbed by the presence of my wife, so my heart becomes absorbed by the loving presence of God (and even more) in contemplative prayer. Thus, contemplative prayer moves from recollection to beholding to an ever-deeper communion with God in the Holy Spirit.

As the work of the Holy Spirit is given more space in the heart, the Holy Spirit raises our hearts' activity — its desires, intercessions, and continued effort to recollect — to a new level. God moves in our hearts, and we cooperate. This cooperation is an intentional offering of the heart. As God warms our hearts in contemplative prayer, He subsequently warms everything inside our hearts, including the petitions we hold there. In this warm grasp, an interior conversation can take place. The words of this conversation are hidden — the language known only by you and God. The hidden communication takes the form of a "heart offering" in which we can give to God our intercessions. Because contemplation is about receiving the gift of God's love through silent communion with Him, we ought to repay Him with the gift of our hearts — including our love and the petitions we hold closely.[22]

---

[22] Also, contemplation is the final phase of prayer within the larger framework of *Lectio Divina* (Divine Reading). *Lectio Divina* is the fourfold method of praying with Sacred Scripture to enter into the deeper presence of God. The structure of *Lectio Divina* is as follows. It begins with *lectio* (reading): the slow, repetitious reading of a specific passage in Scripture in which the soul surrenders to God. This is followed by *meditatio* (meditation): the thoughtful consideration of the selected passage, in which we

If prayer is a "surge of the heart" (Saint Thérèse of Lisieux; CCC 2558), then contemplative prayer is an intense "gushing forth" of love between God and man. Let our intercessory prayer be swept up in this gushing forth!

Rarely do we think about the call and the responsibility of contemplative prayer, but there is much spiritual richness to be found in its practice. The Church encourages us to dive deep into contemplation and become the intercessors that God has intended us to be![23]

Key Patron: Saint John Vianney

The first step in the process for canonization is for the bishop to review the life and writings of the candidate, looking for evidence of virtue and sanctity. Some have suggested that few bishops have ever had it as easy as the bishop of Father John Vianney, the Curé of Ars: the priest's holiness was so renowned. From his calling and formation as a priest, to his battles with the devil, and ultimately

---

allow the Word to be fruitful in our imaginations, memories, and intellects (faculties of the soul) until holy desires are born; the Holy Spirit produces these desires in us because we surrender our internal faculties to the Word. Next is *oratio* (praying): the expression and offering of these holy desires to the Lord, entrusting them to Him and His goodness. When these desires are the intercessions we hold in our hearts, the *oratio* also becomes an important place of intercessory prayer. Lastly, *contemplatio* (contemplation) is the fruition that comes from this holy conversation with God.

[23] Moses was the chief mediator in the Old Testament and offered powerful words of intercessory prayer (see CCC 2574). The prayer of Moses was "characteristic of contemplative prayer by which God's servant remains faithful to his mission" (CCC 2576). Therefore, as Moses shows us, contemplation and intercession belong together.

to his extraordinary love for God and the people he served, Father John Vianney was a man of unwavering commitment to gaining souls for Christ.

Jean-Marie Baptiste Vianney was born in 1786 in France at the dawn of the French Revolution. During this time, the Catholic Church was going through heavy persecution from anti-Catholic civic forces. Political fanatics burned churches and attacked clergy, sending numerous priests to martyrs' deaths.

After receiving his First Communion, young Jean-Marie made his first commitment to Jesus to become a priest, and he later entered the seminary at the age of twenty. His time in formation was quite turbulent. On two occasions, he failed the final exams required for ordination, and his call to the priesthood was put into question. Under the tutelage of Father Balley, a local priest to the seminary, Jean-Marie passed his exams, and on August 13, 1815, at the age of thirty, Jean-Marie became Father Jean-Marie Baptiste Vianney.

Father John Vianney's first assignment was at a parish in a remote village in Ars, France, known for its drunkenness and debauchery. Throughout his time in Ars, the humble parish priest became known for his contemplative prayer, inspirational preaching, and work for the poor. Over the years, he singlehandedly transformed the parish into a place of goodness and conversion.

Father John Vianney's inspirational example upset the forces of evil—and his battles with Satan prove it. Regularly, for thirty-five years (1824–1858), Satan tormented him with wicked voices and evil singing. The demons would drag the humble saint from his bed. Because of this, it was not uncommon for him to go for days without sleep.

Why would Satan target the humble priest of a tiny village with such force? Simply put, Father John Vianney gave 100 percent of his heart to God, 100 percent of the time. He lived for God and others, wholeheartedly, because he prayed to God with all his heart. In other words, his wholehearted intercession was swept up in his devoted contemplation of God. It is the power of Vianney's devotion and intercessory prayer that made him a supreme danger to the devil.

This pious determination to intercede blossomed most fully in his work as a confessor. He took *to heart* the fact that in the confessional others were willing *to share their hearts*. This exposure of the heart before God inspired Father John Vianney to hear confessions for up to sixteen hours a day. Despite the hours he would spend in the confessional, some pilgrims had to wait in three-day-long lines. Many people, from all over the world, flocked to Father Vianney's parish for the opportunity to have their confessions heard by him. It was known that he had received the unique grace of "reading souls"; he could identify specific details about individuals without ever having met them before.

In one case, the story is told:

Mlle. Claudine Venet, of Viregneux, a small village of the canton of Saint-Galmier, in the Loire, was taken to Ars on February 1, 1850. In consequence of an attack of brain fever, she had become completely deaf and blind. M. Vianney had never seen her; no one had introduced her to him. On that February 1, she happened to be standing outside the church as he went by. Without speaking a word, he took her hand, led her into the sacristy and made her kneel down in the confessional. He had hardly given her his blessing when her sight and hearing returned. It seemed to her that she had awakened from a long dream.

After her confession, the servant of God made the following amazing prophecy: "Your eyes are healed, but you will become deaf for another twelve years. It is God's will that it should be so!" On leaving the sacristy, Claudine Venet felt her ears closing once more. As a matter of fact, she could no longer hear anything. The infirmity lasted twelve years as foretold on this February 1, 1850.

Calm and resigned, enjoying the sight that had been restored to her, the stricken woman awaited the day of her deliverance. Great was her emotion when, on January 18, 1862, she felt perfectly cured.[24]

There were many great miracles such as these, but the deeper miracle in each case was the miracle of conversion. When Father John Vianney encountered the heart of another, transformation followed.

What's more, if Father John Vianney sensed an insincere confession, or if he was "reading" lies of the soul, he would weep. On one occasion, he was asked why he wept. He replied, "My friend, I weep because you do not weep."[25] He was grieving the insincerity of others. Indeed, Father John Vianney was blessed, for "blessed are those who mourn, for they shall be comforted" (Matt. 5:4).

Father John Vianney died in the early morning of August 4, 1859. For over a week, thousands of people lined the streets waiting patiently to pay their respects to the man who had touched their lives. The bishop presided over his funeral with an estimated three hundred priests concelebrating Mass and seven thousand people in attendance (there were only two hundred people in the village of Ars when Father John Vianney first arrived as their pastor).

Because the love of God consumed it, the heart of Father John Vianney belonged to the people he served. In 1869, the body, including the heart, of Saint John Vianney was found to be incorrupt.[26] The heart of Saint John Vianney was always *composed* in the

---

[24] Abbe Francois Trochu, *The Cure D'Ars: Saint Jean-Marie-Baptiste Vianney* (New York: TAN Books, 1927), 430.

[25] Ibid, 439.

[26] "The Incorruptibles are saints whose bodies are miraculously preserved after death, defying the normal process of decomposition...."

Spirit. Fittingly then, his heart was without *decomposition*. Today, a reliquary travels the world with the incorrupt heart of Saint John Vianney inside it. Millions have gone to see this great miracle. The world came to encounter the heart of Father John Vianney in the little village of Ars, France. Now, that heart reaches out to the world and continually transforms the lives of many.

Saint John Vianney, pray for us!

Prompt Questions for Journaling

1. When was the last time you have taken someone's prayer request to heart? Why is this important?
2. What gets in the way of your wholehearted prayer? What is the worldly desire that takes away from your 100 percent?

Under usual circumstances, nothing at all has been done to preserve the bodies of these saints. In fact, some of them have been covered in quicklime, which should have easily destroyed any human remains, yet it has no effect of these saints. Many of them also give off a sweet, unearthly odor, and others produce blood or oils that defy any scientific explanation. Modern science relegates the incorruptibles to the status of mummies, pretending it understands and can comfortably categorize these saints. How then do the scientists explain the fact that a year and a half after the death of St. Francis Xavier, a medical examiner placed a finger into one of the saint's wounds and found fresh blood on his finger when he withdrew it? Or that when a finger was amputated from St. John of the Cross several months after his death, it was immediately observed that blood began to flow from the wound? Or the case of St. Nicholas of Tolentino, whose arms have frequently bled over the last 400 years?" "The Incorruptible Saints," Roman Catholic Saints, https://www.roman-catholic-saints.com/incorruptible-saints.html.

4

Pray Fervently

In my two years at Franciscan University of Steubenville in the 1990s, I met lots of people, but the one encounter that made the greatest impression on me was my first meeting with Father Michael Scanlan, T.O.R., who was then the president of the university.

During orientation weekend, each new student had the privilege of meeting Father Mike Scanlan. After the meet and greet, a friar told me that Father Mike wanted to pray over me. I did not hesitate; I went right to him. Before he could say anything, I asked, "Why do you feel called to pray over me?" He responded, "Because the Holy Spirit wanted me to." He then asked me to open my heart to God with the hope the Holy Spirit might "work wonders" in my time at Franciscan University. So that is precisely what I did. I opened my heart.

In the past, I had had people pray over me, but this was different. As Father Mike invoked the presence of the Holy Spirit, I felt the warmth of God's love envelop me. But there was something else too; I was overwhelmed by the sheer holiness of Father Mike and the great fervor with which he prayed.

At that juncture in my life, I was not aware of these words of Saint James: "The fervent prayer of a righteous person is very powerful" (James 5:16, NABRE), but as I look back now, I realize that I have witnessed the truth of the statement. During my time at Franciscan, the Holy Spirit worked wonders in my heart as past wounds were healed and broken relationships were restored. I believe Father Mike had a lot to do with that.

Intercessory Key: Pray Fervently

Fervor is essential to intercessory prayer. We are a result-oriented culture, and intercessory prayer is no different—we want to see its effects. While we are not always granted the privilege of seeing the effects of our prayer, Saint James lets us know that fervent prayer from a man imbued with God's love and grace yields powerful results.

Fervent prayer is a manifestation of praying from the heart. It is the impassioned conviction that arises when it has been set aflame with the fire of God's love. In this earnest prayer, the Holy Spirit, who is the "breath of God" (see John 20:21–22), blows its flames into our hearts, and this produces an intense belief that God will answer us.

Fervent prayer "is powerful in its effects"; it is high-voltage prayer. It puts a charge of spiritual energy into the person for whom we pray. When Jesus prayed with sighs and groans to heal the man with the speech impediment, He was a conduit of energy. We, too, are to become conduits of God's life and of God's energy as we pray fervently.

Tip 1: Remember Who Initiates
Your Life of Intercessory Prayer

As we set out to implement important tips in this key, let us first pause and recall who is operating in our souls. The passage in James in its larger context (5:16–18) can help us:

Therefore, confess your sins to one another and pray for one another, that you may be healed. The fervent prayer of a righteous person is very powerful. Elijah was a human being like us; yet he prayed earnestly that it might not rain, and for three years and six months it did not rain upon the land. Then he prayed again, and the sky gave rain and the earth produced its fruit.

For many souls, the mere mention of the name Elijah conjures up all sorts of emotions tied to the awe-inspiring power of God. Is this why James presents fervent prayer within the context of Elijah? Partly.

Before James comments on the success of Elijah's fervent prayer, he reminds us that Elijah was "a human being like us." Although remembered for his miracles, Elijah also experienced many hardships in his life, including deep anguish and torment (see 1 Kings 19:4). By referencing Elijah's "humanness" right before the power of his fervent prayer, James highlights the role of the Holy Spirit in Elijah's miracles. It was the Holy Spirit that moved Elijah's heart to intercede on behalf of the chosen people. Elijah did not conjure up some magical potion and call down God; rather, God came down into his soul and inspired him to cry out for divine help. At this moment, James wants us to see that we, who are human beings like Elijah, can do "unbelievable" things in the name of God and in cooperation with the Holy Spirit.[27] As Saint James tells us, it was the power of God moving in Elijah's earnest, steadfast, fervent prayer that commanded authority over the rain. When he prayed for the rain to stop, it stopped; when he prayed for the rain to continue, it continued (see James 5:17–18).

[27] See Daniel A. Keating and Kelly Anderson, *Catholic Commentary on Sacred Scripture: James, First, Second, and Third John* (Grand Rapids, MI: Baker Academic, 2017), 117–118.

Unleashing the Power of Intercessory Prayer

Fervent prayer should never be reduced to some hyper-emotional, fancy-worded prayer. Although the Holy Spirit does inspire passion and words of articulation, it ought to be stirred up authentically by Him. To invite this "stirring up" to take place in our lives, we ought to beg the Holy Spirit to move our hearts.

Tip 2: Beg, Hunger, Thirst

Begging is more than asking; it involves something deeper, a craving. To ask is to want; to beg is to crave. Jesus says "knock" (Matt. 7:7), and in our craving, we bang down the door. While one can translate prayer as "asking," James wants us to see that fervent prayer comes from a deeper place and thus needs to be expressed through "begging."

In James 5:16, the Greek word for "prayer," *deomai*, translates as "a begging that arises from union with God." In principle, fervent prayer comes from the depths of the heart, a passionate cry for the intervention of God—a begging, a holy craving. Think of the occurrences in your life when you cried out to God for His intervention. I mean, really cried! That's *deomai*! When Jesus prayed this way, He sweat blood (see Luke 22:44). It does not get any more intense, or fervent, than that.

Some Bibles use the terms "earnest" and "steadfast" to describe fervent prayer.[28] In our intercessory prayer, when we long for God the same way our lungs long for air, the fruit of that prayer is a growing desire to see it answered. Just as the thirsty person begs for a drink until his thirst is quenched, so a praying person begs for a petition until it is answered.

---

[28] New American Bible: "fervent prayer"; New Living Translation, Catholic Edition: "earnest prayer"; Douay-Rheims Bible: "continual prayer"; Knox translation: "prays fervently."

We see this kind of steadfast prayer in the parable of the widow and the unrighteous judge (see Luke 18:1–8). In effect, Jesus tells His listeners not to grow weary of praying. In the parable, the widow was constant in her pleading for justice as she "continually" went before the unjust judge, seeking vindication. Eventually, the judge exonerated the vulnerable widow. Jesus closes the parable with some powerful words: "Pay close attention to what the dishonest judge says. Will not God then secure the rights of the chosen ones who call out to him day and night? Will he be slow to answer them? He will see to it that justice is done to them speedily" (Luke 18:6–8). Essentially, Jesus says to us: "If a dishonest judge grants the requests of a widow's relentless plea, how much more will my Father in heaven grant your relentless intercessory prayer!"

We see this same relentless prayer in Amalek's defeat at the "hands" of Moses. What do we read in the book of Exodus? "Whenever Moses held up his hand, Israel prevailed; and whenever he lowered his hand, Amalek prevailed" (Exod. 17:11). To secure victory, when Moses' hands grew weary, Aaron and Hur propped up his arms on a stone and held up his hands (see Exod. 17:12). Israel's victory hinged on the intercessory prayer of Moses and the others (Aaron and Hur) who came to his aid. God desires that we lift our hands in the same fervent prayer — hungering and thirsting for God to intervene in the situation we are praying for.

Since fervent prayer shoots forth from "righteousness" (James 5:16), we ought to consider its relationship to the corresponding beatitude: "Blessed are those who hunger and thirst for righteousness, for they will be satisfied" (Matt. 5:6). Hunger for food and thirst for water are the most basic expressions of human need; each conveys a consuming desire. Jesus employs these terms to correlate appetite with beatitude. In doing so, we ought to ask certain questions:

- When was the last time I was hungry or thirsty?
- Did my hunger and thirst become my preoccupation?
- To what lengths did I go to have my "fill"?

After asking yourselves these questions, apply your reflection on hunger and thirst to your walk with God, asking another question: "Do I hunger and thirst for God as much as I ought?" The psalmist might help us here: "As the deer longs for streams of water, so my soul longs for you, O God" (Ps. 42:2). Do we echo the psalmist's ache for righteousness?

What is righteousness? Righteousness is to be *right* with God. The righteous man conforms his mind and heart to the objective truth of God. Righteousness is holiness. Holiness is to walk uprightly in the presence of God. This kind of godly walk sets us apart. In fact, the Hebrew word for holiness, *qadosh*, means "to be set apart" or "dedicated" to God (see Lev. 26:12). The more we conform our lives to the objective revelation of God, the more we will be "set apart" from a world that increasingly distances itself from divine revelation and objective truth. Holiness is light. The darker it gets around us, the brighter our light shines.

Since "God is a consuming fire" (Heb. 12:29), it could be said that when God has consumed man, he has been set on fire. Certainly, Elijah was a man of righteousness, set on fire for God by God. He begged, hungered, and thirsted for God, and as he did, his deep craving yielded great power in its effects.

Fervent prayer changes things: it heals hearts, aids in the process of reconciliation, helps us overcome temptation, strengthens the weak, and even cures illnesses. Fervent prayer can do all of this because it is the power of God in you. The Spirit that brought forth creation and hovered above the waters in the book of Genesis is the same powerful Spirit that is inside you when you pray for another. The power of God in you is the power to emit light into the person for whom or the circumstance for which you are praying.

Tip 3: Emit Solar Flares!

Scientists tell us that the sun is an estimated 5,778 degrees Celsius. This great solar ball of energy occasionally sends off flares, which are brief eruptions of intense high-energy radiation from its surface, often causing electromagnetic disturbances on the earth. When a man has been consumed by God's divine fire of love in the Holy Spirit (a love hotter than 5,778 degrees Celsius), he, too, emits a sudden brightness of light, often disturbing earth's inhabitants (see Acts 2:1–14).

To be fervent is not only to be on fire for God but also to emit the power of God. This happens when His high-energy radiation touches us.[29] Among other things, this emittance includes enthusiasm and joy.

In the spiritual life, enthusiasm — often correlated with fervency — is a great solar flare that manifests the life of God within. Enthusiasm comes from the Greek word *en-theos*, which translates as "to bear God within." Quite literally, the enthusiastic soul for Christ is a "God-bearer." Every saint is a God-bearer — a revelation of God's dynamic light-bearing love. Enthusiasm, then, is the manifestation of an interior spark brought about by the Holy Spirit, who is God's energy. This enthusiasm expresses itself in conviction and zeal for God — being on fire in God and for God. We can see this principle in a secular context. When someone is very enthusiastic about a team, he experiences a zealous devotion to it. Often, this devotion manifests itself in "brief eruptions" of cheering for the team for which he is rooting (at least this is what happens to me when I watch Notre Dame football). The soul who is enthusiastic about Christ is devoted to Him and, at times, briefly erupts for Him.

---

[29] The disciples on the Road to Emmaus found their hearts "burning within" (Luke 24:32) because their hearts had encountered the great solar flare of the resurrected Christ.

Unleashing the Power of Intercessory Prayer

Enthusiasm is a flare of grace-filled joy. Joy is a fruit of the Holy Spirit, a strong light, and a grace that dispels darkness. "Joy" and "grace" share the same Greek root, *charis*, implying that joy *is* grace. In other words, as grace inhabits the soul, so does the delight to pray for others abide in our wanting to fulfill God's will.

Joy and enthusiasm are markers of the fervent saint, the holy one of God who has been set on fire for Him. The fervent soul is always emitting solar flares that bring about powerful effects. In intercessory prayer, joy and enthusiasm set afire our zeal to pray earnestly for the other because we know that God loves this person and desires his good. Intercessory prayer shouldn't be passionless; rather, it should burst forth from that fire of God within us, joy.

In the end, fervent prayer is a life filled with the fire of the Holy Spirit, expressing itself in a persevering earnestness, a passionate cry, and at times, enthusiastic, joy-filled energy — always effective in its results. Prayer without fervor is like the sun without energy and heat. Therefore, we must pray with fervency.

Key Patron: Saint Monica of Hippo

It has been said, "Behind every great man, you can always find a great woman." We know Saint Augustine as one of the greatest saints of the Catholic Church because of his dramatic conversion from playboy to priest and his renowned scholarship on Catholic doctrine. But to know the life and times of this saint is to encounter the woman behind it all: Saint Monica. In many respects, everything we admire about Saint Augustine's greatness is owed to Saint Monica — not by simply being his mother, but by her virtuous discipline of fervent prayer for her son. By Saint Augustine's own account, it was because of the great love of Monica and her passionate prayer for him that he would find himself in the arms of God.

A reading of Saint Monica's life reveals that she devoted much time at the altar of intercession, begging God to intervene on behalf of those whom she loved. Customary to the time and place she lived (early fourth century in North Africa), when Monica was of marriageable age, it was arranged for her to marry the pagan Patricius. Known for his anger and criticism of Christianity, Patricius was intolerable, but Monica saw this as her cross, and with committed prayer, she patiently interceded for the conversion of her husband. A year before he died, he converted to the Christian faith. In his classic *Confessions*, Saint Augustine had particular praise for her virtuous approach with Patricius.[30]

Patricius's mother was equally insufferable. This did not deter the pious Monica from fervent prayer for her as well, and Patricius's mother, too, converted to the Christian faith before she passed away. Monica's exemplary prayer life had a significant impact on all her children, including Navigius and Perpetua. By all accounts, Navigius lived a noble life, one worthy of imitation, and Perpetua devoted hers to fervent intercessory prayer by becoming a religious.

Augustine's wayward behavior in his earlier years tested Monica's devotion to God.[31] In a touchstone moment in her life, after weeping greatly for Augustine's embrace of the heresy Manicheism and his life of debauchery, she had a vision of a mysterious figure. As she was weeping, she looked up, and from this indistinct figure came a voice saying, "Monica, dry your tears, your son is with you."[32] The words brought great comfort to the suffering mother and left a lasting impression upon her. Indeed, Augustine was in the deepest place of Monica's heart, in the fervent offering of her powerful prayer, which would soon bring about his conversion.

---

[30] Augustine, *Confessions* (London: Penguin Classics, 1961), bk. 9.

[31] Ibid.

[32] Ibid.

Monica would follow Augustine in his travels, imploring him to abandon his errant ways. Eventually, in Milan, Monica entered into spiritual direction under Saint Ambrose. He counseled her to stay steadfast in her prayers, assuring her that God would answer. On one occasion, he told her, "It is not possible that the son of so many tears should perish."[33] As it turns out, that same Saint Ambrose was catechizing Augustine in the Christian faith, and on Easter in the year 387, Augustine was received into the Catholic Church.

Clearly, Saint Monica was emitting solar flares. Her fervent prayer brought about the conversions of her husband, her mother-in-law, and her son and inspired upright behavior in her two other children. Her deep hunger and thirst to see those whom she loved baptized and consecrated to God make up the entire story of her life. In fact, toward the end of her life — after Augustine had converted to Christianity — she struggled to understand why she was still alive. In her own words, "I do not know what there is left for me to do or why I am still here, all my hopes in this world being now fulfilled. All I wished for was that I might see you a Catholic and a child of heaven. God granted me even more than this in making you despise earthly felicity and consecrate yourself to His service."[34] Monica would die soon after these words were spoken in 387.

The Church has declared Saint Monica the patron saint for converting sinners because she devoted her life to interceding with a resolute heart for others, often praying into the night. If your prayer request is for the conversion of a particular soul, then Saint Monica is your gal! We call upon her intercession in this fourth key, praying fervently, because her brave heart and undying faithfulness define what lies behind the *deomai*. She was in union

[33] Ibid.
[34] Ibid.

with God, crying out to Him to transform the heart of her son. God heard her cry (see Job 34:28), and Augustine has emerged as truly one of the greatest saints of the Catholic Church. Monica lived her vocation to pray intensely for others. Ask her for guidance in your own prayer—and pray fervently!

Saint Monica, pray for us!

Prompt Questions for Journaling

1. Do you hunger and thirst to see God work in the life of the one whom you are praying for? Why or why not?
2. What in the life of Saint Monica encourages you to pray more fervently? Reflect.

5

Pray on the Spot

In the summer of 2018, I had the blessed opportunity to dine with Dan Burke and Deacon Colin Coleman, the founder of and a professor with the Avila Institute, respectively. As we shared our stories and talked about spiritual theology, our conversation narrowed on the topic of deliverance ministry, specifically for those struggling with addiction and mental illnesses.

As the conversation went deeper, Dan Burke stopped me and asked, "Can we pray for what is on your heart right now?"

"Yes," I said.

Deacon Coleman then put his hand on my shoulder, and we began to pray. The three of us prayed intently over that dining room table for the souls on my heart. It was consoling as I felt the presence of God in our midst. Indeed, "where two or three are gathered in my name, there am I in the midst of them" (Matt. 18:20). There is always strength in numbers!

As I look back on my encounter with Dan and Deacon Coleman, I recall being filled with more than just food: I was filled with the Holy Spirit. These two souls for Christ saw the need for prayer and prayed with *urgency* for God's intervention. Their prayer did not say, "I'll pray for you later, at some future time" — no. They prayed right there at the dining table. Dan and Deacon Coleman saw time as a gift — for judgment awaits us, and we need to see the present moment as the only gift of which we can be assured. Time itself is the great gift from God.

Intercessory Key: Pray on the Spot

As we say, "Yes, I will pray for you" with a spiritual fervor and faith-filled heart, we ought to do so on the spot. We should not waste time, "for salvation is nearer to us now than when we first believed" (Rom. 13:11). Time is precious. Tomorrow is not guaranteed. Saint Paul "urged" Timothy to offer up prayers of intercession for him (see 1 Tim 2:1-5). He also "urged" the Roman faithful to earnestly pray for him (see Rom 15:30). He did so because intercessory prayer is a pressing matter!

In addition to the value of the present moment, praying on the spot brings about the presence of God (see Matt. 18:20) and assures the individuals in need that you are serious about praying for them. This is both encouraging and enriching for the souls who witness it.

Spontaneous prayer arises from the heart of contemplation. The more we withdraw into the deep caverns of our hearts, the greater the desire we will have to intercede on the spot.

Tip 1: Now Is the Right Time to Connect with the Timeless

As a parent, I have the pleasure of watching my four children open gifts five times a year (birthdays and Christmas). Each year, I watch my children spend more time playing with the bubble wrap than with the gift inside the wrapping. Often, the gift ends up being put aside to be played with another day. It is usually at this point that I turn to my wife and ask, "Why did we not just put bubble wrap in an empty box?" Not only would the kids have been just as happy, but a lot of money would have been saved. (My wife and I are slowly learning our lesson here.)

Pray on the Spot

In the most recent opening of gifts, I asked myself another question. In what ways have I been "putting aside" what God has gifted to me? After due reflection, the one word that was ringing in my ear was "time." Time is the one thing we tend to ignore as a gift. Time can never be replaced. Most gifts we receive can either be exchanged or returned, but time is different—we can never get it back. For this reason, praying on the spot is an excellent use of our time and is quintessential to intercessory prayer.

To invite the Holy Spirit into someone's need is to have the Holy Spirit move into that need—not tomorrow, but today, in the here and now. Next time you are asked, "Will you pray for me?" respond with prayer and watch the good Lord work in the here and now.

I tend to say, "There are not enough hours in the day to get to everything"—which indicates that I need to adjust my perspective on time. God got it right when He created the twenty-four-hour day. Generally, the more I pray, the less time is a burden, and the more I pray with others, the more it helps them overcome seeing time as a burden as well. Typically, when we pray with others, the Holy Spirit overshadows that prayer with a calming presence. In this way, praying on the spot is invaluable to intercessory prayer.

Unfortunately, when we are asked to pray for someone, we often hastily agree to do so but forget the paramount task that we took upon ourselves—praying for a soul in need. Imagine, when was the last time you stopped what you were doing, surrendered your time, and prayed for the soul who asked you to pray for him or her? To do so is to have a tremendous impact upon the soul for whom you are praying. Personally, when Dan Burke and Deacon Coleman prayed with me at that meal, I was changed for the better. God's grace invaded my day, and I was more whole because of it. If we are in the habit of "rushing to the next thing," we don't engage in intercessory prayer as we ought. We should slow down, recollect, and reexamine our prayer lives. If we are going to pray better on the spot, we need to be better about making prayer the center of our lives. The absence of a constant prayer life will lead to the absence of following through on prayer requests. We would be deeply offended by God if we thought He was not following through on our prayer requests, and we ought to treat others as we would like to be treated. The Golden Rule applies here in spades.

As we reflect on time, we can benefit greatly by considering the words of the preacher in Ecclesiastes:

> Vanity of vanities, says the Preacher,
> vanity of vanities! All is vanity ...
> All things are full of weariness;
> a man cannot utter it;
> the eye is not satisfied with seeing,
> nor the ear filled with hearing.
> What has been is what will be,
> and what has been done is what will be done;
> and there is nothing new under the sun.
> Is there a thing of which it is said,
> "See, this is new"?
> It has been already,
> in the ages before us.
> There is no remembrance of former things,
> nor will there be any remembrance
> of later things yet to happen
> among those who come after. (1:2–11)

While the word "vanity" typically recalls excessive attention to one's physical appearance, the Latin, *vanitatem*, best translates as "aimlessness" or "worthlessness." The danger of vanity is not necessarily in the superficial trappings, but rather in our obsessions that lead to significant waste in time — time that is idle and void of any meaning.[35] The preacher's lesson is this: a life without a mind for the infinite is "full of weariness" (Eccles. 1:8). Without the advent of Christ in our hearts, our finite ways of thinking and use of time are without aim, futile, and worthless. With the advent of Christ, and the gift of grace that our souls receive, our new ways of thinking stretch to the infinite and our prayer gains more purpose.

Ultimately, how we use the finite gift of time determines how much fruit our intercessory prayer will bring forth. Making a point to pray for others on the spot, and generally to pray more for others daily, is a good place to start. Since we know not the day nor the hour (see Matt. 24:36), we remain vigilant in "devoted prayer" (see Rom. 12:12).

One way to live our lives, given God's time, is to *pray for the living and the dead* and to *comfort the sorrowful*.

Tip 2: Work Mercifully

Mercy is usually equated with reaching out to the homeless at soup kitchens or donating clothes to children's charities. Rarely do we equate mercy with prayer and being present to others spiritually.[36]

---

[35] See Hollcraft, *A Heart for Evangelizing*, 17.

[36] According to our Lord's private revelations given to Saint Faustina Kowalska in 1931, Jesus spoke of three ways to exercise mercy toward our neighbors. "The first—by deed, the second—by word, the third—by prayer." Holy Mother Church has identified fourteen corporal (deed) and spiritual (word) works of mercy (see footnote 20). Inside the seven spiritual works of mercy is the one spiritual work of *praying for the living and the dead*. According to Jesus, this spiritual work of prayer should be held in the highest regard: "Many souls ... are often worried because they do not have the material means with which to carry out an act of mercy. Yet spiritual mercy, which requires neither permissions nor storehouses, is much more

Unleashing the Power of Intercessory Prayer

As we continue to consider this key of praying on the spot, I thought it would be helpful to consider the deep spiritual bond that exists between two of the seven spiritual works of mercy: *pray for the living and the dead* and *comfort the sorrowful.* In my experience, the fear of losing someone often prompts us to pray for that person in the here and now. I don't think there is any request with greater urgency than to pray for someone who has passed away and to pray with and be present to the grieving.

Death is very difficult for most people. And when we lose someone close to us, we want to say that that person is "in a better place"—heaven. However, how can we know that for certain? Without some mystical vision, we cannot possibly know where that person is. Saint Paul tells us that, unless we die in mortal sin, heaven is our destiny—but not before being purified in the fire of God's love. "If any man's work is burned up, he will suffer loss, though he himself will be saved, but only as through fire" (1 Cor. 3:15). In reflecting upon these verses, Pope Emeritus Benedict XVI states: "It is in any case evident that our salvation can take different forms, that some of what is built may be burned down, that in order to be saved we personally have to pass through 'fire' so as to become fully open to receiving God and able to take our place at the table of the eternal marriage-feast."[37] In Saint Peter's first letter, we read, "... so that the genuineness of your faith, more precious than gold which though perishable is tested by fire, may redound to praise and glory and honor at the revelation of Jesus Christ" (1

---

meritorious and is within the grasp of every soul." Saint Maria Faustina Kowalska, *Divine Mercy in My Soul: The Diary of the Servant of God, Sister M. Faustina Kowalska* (Stockbridge, MA: Marian Press, 1987), no. 1317.

[37] Pope Benedict XVI, Encyclical Letter on Christian Hope *Spe Salvi* (November 30, 2007), no. 46.

Pet. 1:7). Sacred Tradition calls this purification by fire purgatory because our souls are purged of their impurities (see CCC 1472).

Biblical evidence for praying for the dead is found as far back as the book of Maccabees, in which Judas Maccabeus prays for Jewish soldiers who have been slain (2 Mac. 12:38–46). Saint Paul also prays for the deceased (see 2 Tim 1:18). Throughout the sacred history of the Christian faith, people have followed the pattern of Saint Paul and Judas Maccabeus to pray for the living *and the dead*. We pray for the souls of the departed because they are suffering, and where there is suffering, there should always be intercessory prayer.[38] We pray for the living *and the dead* because souls are suffering, but they are not the only souls suffering; the people left behind are suffering as well.

People who lose loved ones go through a grieving process. Grief is messy, and that's okay. Grief has no planned start or finish, and that's okay. Most of us have mourned the loss of someone close to us, and we are all too familiar with this unplanned messiness. Hence the call to comfort the sorrowful by praying with them and accompanying them in their grieving process. This calls for the pastoral gift of personal accompaniment.

Personal accompaniment is journeying with others to bring them into full communion with Jesus Crist. Accompaniment calls for the virtues of gentleness, compassion, and silence. Gentleness is the virtue of calmness—the soft action or light touch that assists in the process of healing. Compassion is the "suffering with" (*cum-passio*)—the deep warmth that carries with it the gift of charity. Silence is the quieting of the mind and the slow movement of the heart that seeks to engage the grieving hearts. In this space, we

---

[38] Here, I highly recommend the Chaplet of Divine Mercy. For a step-by-step guide on how to pray the chaplet, see "How to Recite the Chaplet," The Divine Mercy, https://www.thedivinemercy.org/message/devotions/pray-the-chaplet.

understand that the best thing we can do is often the only thing we can do — weep with others.

As exemplified by Charlie Brown, we say "good grief" when we are exacerbated, but there is — quite literally — a grief that *is* good when we are grieving with others. Weeping ought to be holy. "Jesus wept" (John 11:35). Saint Paul says, "Weep with those who weep" (Rom. 12:15). When we intentionally offer our tears to God, we offer up a powerful intercessory prayer — "bearing another's burdens, and so fulfilling the law of Christ" (Gal. 6:2).

Given these two spiritual works of mercy, we should also be aware of the importance of prayer as a source of communion. In many cases, to pray with others bestows a real sense of belonging, and this itself can be a great source of consolation.

The seventeenth-century Italian painter Guercino is arguably most famous for his piece *Saint Peter Weeping before the Virgin*. It is a deeply moving work that shows Mary at the side of Peter, who is lamenting the three times that he denied knowing Christ. On the right of the portrait is Peter hunching down with a handkerchief over his eyes, grieving. On the left is Mary, a portrait of one who perfectly comforts the sorrowful. With her hands folded around a second handkerchief, she is hunched over, with her body turned toward Peter. Mary appears gentle, compassionate, and as one who is quietly praying for the grieving Peter. I encourage you to find this painting online and ponder it as a reminder of what this great work of mercy is about: a profound, yet quiet movement of the Holy Spirit prompting the heart to work mercifully by being present, by praying on the spot.

Key Patron: Saint Pio of Pietrelcina

Humanity is always fascinated by the supernatural, so when we come across the likes of a Saint Padre Pio of Pietrelcina, we often fixate on that which cannot be explained by science. From the stories of his bilocation and his ability to heal the sick, to his receiving the stigmata and his visions of heavenly hosts,[39] the life of Saint Padre Pio makes for fascinating dinnertime conversation. Underneath the mystical phenomena, however, was a man who saw time as a gift, an opportunity to pray more and to work mercifully. In the words of Saint John Paul II, spoken during the canonization of Padre Pio, "prayer and charity are the most concrete syntheses of Padre Pio's teaching."

Francesco Forgione (Padre Pio) was born into a poor, Catholic family in 1887 in Pietrelcina, Italy. From his earliest days, Francesco saw the preciousness of time, as he suffered a great deal. A sickly child, he almost died of typhoid fever. At the age of seventeen, he dealt with agonizing pain in his digestive tract (at one point, only being able to digest milk and cheese). He battled these health issues up to and through his ordination in 1910. In 1915, Padre Pio joined the Italian Army. Only one year later, it was believed that he had tuberculosis, and he was discharged from military service.[40]

Padre Pio's prolonged battle with his health would prepare him for what would eventually launch him onto the world stage in the fall of 1918. On September 20, 1918, after having celebrated Mass, he was in a prayer of thanksgiving when he suddenly had a vision. In his own words from a letter to his spiritual director:

[39] Padre Pio experienced the supernatural phenomena of bilocation — the mystical gift of being in two places at once (as testified to by his fellow friars); the stigmata — the marks corresponding to the Passion of Christ that are impressed upon the flesh by divine favor (the blood that came from the wounds of Padre Pio was said to have smelled like roses or a sweet-smelling perfume); the gift of reading souls — the extraordinary charism of identifying specific details about individuals without ever having met them; and on numerous occasions he saw Jesus, Mary, and the guardian angels.

[40] Although he had chronic coughs and high fevers, it was never confirmed that he had tuberculosis.

Unleashing the Power of Intercessory Prayer

It all happened in a flash.... I saw before me a mysterious Person, similar to the one I had seen on August 5th, differing only because His hands, feet and side were dripping blood. The sight of Him frightened me: what I felt at that moment is indescribable. I thought I would die, and would have died if the Lord hadn't intervened and strengthened my heart which was about to burst out of my chest. The Person disappeared and I became aware that my hands, feet and side were pierced and were dripping with blood.[41]

"In a flash," the young padre, thirty-one years of age, received the stigmata. His life of suffering now culminated in the wounds of Calvary, but for this Italian priest, his Calvary would last fifty years. He died in 1968. Thousands attended his funeral.

Saint Padre Pio's long *via dolorosa* sharpened his understanding of the value of time. On one occasion, he exclaimed, "Oh, how precious time is! Blessed are those who know how to make good use of it. Oh, if only all could understand how precious time is, undoubtedly everyone would do his best to spend it in a praiseworthy manner!" For Padre Pio, what was worthy of praise was "prayer and charity."

Prayer, specifically intercessory prayer, dominated the life of Padre Pio. (At the conclusion of this book you will find the prayer Padre Pio prayed every day that led to so many miracles.) He would receive hundreds of prayer requests every day, often by mail. Heeding his counsel to others, he never put off prayer from one moment to another because he understood that "the [next moment] is not yet ours."[42] As we have highlighted, this lesson on prayer is invaluable to our petitions of intercession. We cannot put off prayer for

---

[41] Padre Pio, *Epistolario*, vol. 1, no 1093, letter dated October 22, 1983.
[42] "Some of Padre Pio's Quotes," Padre Pio Foundation, http://www.padrepiofoundation.com/Padre_Pio_quotes.htm.

another time because that time is never guaranteed—only the moment that is before us.

What's more, Padre Pio was a man of spontaneous prayer for others. Let me give you one example. In 1967, shortly before Padre Pio's death, John Paul II, then Archbishop Karol Wojtyla of Krakow, sent a letter to Padre Pio, asking him to pray for Wanda Poltawska, a friend and professor at Krakow University who was seriously ill with throat cancer. It was revealed to Karol Wojtyla that Padre Pio, immediately after receiving the letter, took this request to prayer and prayed to God with great intensity for her healing. She was inexplicably healed of her throat cancer soon after that. Wanda had the blessed opportunity to go on a pilgrimage to San Giovanni Rotundo and meet the man who prayed for her. She was also present at his canonization on June 16, 2002.

One of the charisms of Padre Pio's intercessory prayer was his love for the holy souls in purgatory. Having been given the gift of visiting souls in purgatory, Padre Pio understood the importance of praying for the living *and the dead*. He told stories of souls from purgatory coming to visit him, especially during Mass. In one case, he told a friar that "more souls of the dead than of the living climb this mountain to attend my Masses and to seek my prayers."[43] When we pray for the holy souls in purgatory, we would be well served to call upon the intercession of the great Saint Padre Pio.[44]

---

[43] Maura Roan McKeegan, "Padre Pio, Purgatory, and Praying for Souls in the Cemetery," *Catholic Exchange*, October 31, 2017, https://catholicexchange.com/padre-pio-purgatory-praying-souls -cemetery.

[44] Saint Pio offers us extraordinary evidence of the Mass's redeeming power—an affirmation of what the Church has taught from her earliest days. In the sixth century, Pope Saint Gregory the Great wrote, "The holy Sacrifice of Christ, our saving victim, brings great benefits to souls even after death, provided their sins can be pardoned in the life to come. For this reason, souls of the dead

Unleashing the Power of Intercessory Prayer

What's more, Padre Pio's spiritual counsel to the sorrowful and downtrodden was not limited to the confessional. In 1946, with the support of Padre Pio, the House for the Alleviation of Suffering was built on nearby Mount Gargano. There Padre Pio continued his ministry of comforting the sorrowful.

Many people traveled from all over the world to visit and encounter the supernatural that was attributed to Padre Pio and left struck by his holiness. For it was in his holy willingness to pray with them that they found consolation and hope. May we find that same consolation and hope as we turn to Saint Padre Pio to help us to be more vigilant in our response to the question "Will you pray for me?"

Saint Padre Pio, pray for us!

Prompt Questions for Journaling

1. When was the last time you stopped what you were doing, surrendered your time, and prayed for the soul who asked you to pray for him or her?
2. Do you exercise the spiritual works of mercy to pray for the living and the dead and to comfort the sorrowful? Reflect.

---

sometimes beg to have Masses said for them." See Gregory the Great, *Dialogues*, trans. John Zimmerman, OSB (Washington D.C: Catholic University of America Press 1959), 266. The words of Pope Gregory the Great and the experience of Saint Pio ought to have us rushing to have Masses said for our loved ones.

6

Pray with Specifics

The summer before my senior year of high school, my friend and I set out for a seven-hour road trip to the coast of Southern California. This trip included going through the Grapevine, a canyon of approximately forty miles that connects Central California (the Valley) and Southern California. At specific stretches of this pass, there is nothing but open road, and sure enough, during one of these stretches, our car broke down. It was 2:00 in the afternoon, over one hundred degrees, and it was 1992—before cell phones. Although we put our emergency lights on, no one was interested in stopping to assist us. Overcome with anxiety, we began to pray.

My friend grew up in a devout Baptist family. I was raised Catholic. At this moment, we both started to pray, but we did so differently. I prayed, "God, please help us in our time of need. We don't have any other place to turn—" and my friend interrupted me, praying fervently, "Sweet Jesus, please send us someone who knows what is wrong with our engine so that we can get back on the road." This prayer struck me. It not only came from a place of great faith and confidence in God, but it was so specific. Minutes later, a car mechanic "happened" to stop at the side of the road with all the tools needed. It was our alternator. He fixed it, and we were on our way. As we drove off, my friend made the observation: "Why do you pray to God as if you don't know Him? You need to be more intentional when you pray. Doesn't Jesus want specifics?" My friend was right, and that day, not only was an alternator repaired, but so was my understanding of how we ought to pray—intentionally and with specifics.

Intercessory Key: Pray with Specifics

Don't be generic before God! He desires to know the details of what is in our hearts—this is not for His sake (He already knows the details) but for ours. As a father, I rejoice when my child is detailed in his requests. It shows me that he knows what he wants. God rejoices over the same deliberate prayer. Be intentional in your intercessory prayer: turn your attention exclusively toward God and be specific in your petition. Jesus desires as much.

Few passages sound the alarm more clearly for the need to be specific in prayer than the healing of Bartimaeus in Mark 10:46–52. We read:

> And they came to Jericho.... Bartimaeus, a blind beggar, the son of Timaeus, was sitting by the roadside. And when he heard that it was Jesus of Nazareth, he began to cry out and say, "Jesus, Son of David, have mercy on me!" And many rebuked him, telling him to be silent; but he cried out all the more, "Son of David, have mercy on me!" And Jesus stopped and said, "Call him." And they called the blind man, saying to him, "Take heart; rise, he is calling you." And throwing off his mantle he sprang up and came to Jesus. And Jesus said to him, "What do you want me to do for you?" And the blind man said to him, "Master, let me receive my sight." And Jesus said to him, "Go your way; your faith has made you well." And immediately he received his sight and followed him on the way.

In this narrative, Bartimaeus hears Jesus from a curbside and cries out to Him for mercy—twice. Jesus stops, calls him forth, and asks him point-blank, "What do you want me to do for you?" Bartimaeus asked Jesus for mercy, and Jesus hearing his cry, asks him to be more specific.[45]

Tip 1: Be Personal

I will be brief on this tip because it is at the center of our key in the next chapter.

Ambiguities are impersonal. Details are personal. The less we "hide" from Jesus in prayer, the more intimate our friendship with Jesus will become. As a friend, Jesus desires to "go into" our hearts (see Rev. 3:20) and into the minute details of our every need. Jesus asks the disciples on the road to Emmaus, "What things are troubling you?" because He wants us to articulate the particulars in our hearts (see Luke 24:13–35). And He wants us, in doing so, to lay our hearts bare before Him—again, not for His sake but for ours.

The more personal and detailed our prayer, the easier we will identify what is from God versus what is from man. For example, when we ask God to help us win the lottery, and He asks us, "Why?" we might soon realize that such a request is less about God's will and more about our immediate gratification. Intercessory prayer is not

---

[45] Bartimaeus cried out: "I want to see!" He could have otherwise said, "I want to be known." Faith is a desire to see, which is the more profound desire to be known—to see and be seen is to be known. Only the Spirit of God can make our hearts fully known to us (see CCC, 2563). Bartimaeus's desire to see points to another truth. We all have "blind spots": the inability to see how God works in each circumstance and situation. Our intercessory prayer ought to include the prayer "I want to see"—that we will come to see the often unseen movement of God.

rubbing the genie lamp and getting whatever we want, although we may treat it that way. This point is uber-important because, behind it, Jesus asks, "What motivates your prayer?" God questions us, "Is what you ask of me for the glory of man or the glory of God?"

In our intercessory prayer, Jesus asks us the same question He asked Bartimaeus, "What do you want me to do for you?" The Savior of the world is madly in love with you, and He desires to help you. So He emphasizes the prayer of personalism: "What do *you* want *me* to do *for you*." Our God is not some impersonal force in an unreachable space; He is the God of personalism, the God of the living—"flesh ... dwelling among us" (John 1:14). How consoling is it that God says to us: "What do *you* want *me* to do *for you*?" We must return such personalism with equal personalism: "I desire *you* to [fill in the blank] for *my* brother [sister, friend, and so forth], but only as it *gives You glory*." What's more, Sacred Scripture exhorts us to "find the grace" for those who are "in need" (Heb. 4:16). Where do we search for such grace? The "throne of grace" (Heb. 4:16)—the holy of holies, which has been opened by the sacrifice of Christ to unleash the power of grace through intercessory prayer.

As your request is made known to God, let your request be known to others and mobilize a spiritual army of prayer warriors to join you in your explicit prayer of intercession. Ask priests to say Mass for the petition (more on this chapter 8), call friends to pray the Chaplet of Divine Mercy at three o'clock, dedicate family Rosaries, and so forth. Unless the prayer request calls for prudential silence, summon the people of God to storm heaven with prayers. Let Jesus know what we desire Him to do! The soul that begs, hungers, and thirsts for God (as discussed in chapter 4) does not hesitate to assemble an army of intercessors!

Furthermore, I believe it is highly powerful to pray for another before ourselves. When my children come to me, and I initiate the conversation by asking, "What do you want me to do for you?" and my children respond not with what they want, but with what their siblings want—I, as their father, am thrilled. When we place our brothers and sisters in Christ before ourselves, God the Father is overjoyed!

Jesus wants us to know that He will meet our deepest desires. God's deepest desire is that we desire Him as much as He desires us. Specific prayer is personal prayer because we examine ourselves, our deepest desires, and persevere in asking God to reveal Himself in our petition. We search our hearts and pray with fervent desire.

And yes, God's answer might be "no" or "not yet" (as previously discussed), but that should not discourage us from praying with specifics because Jesus, and His great apostle Paul, ask us to do as much. Prayer is less about what God needs to *hear* and more about what we need to *say*. God doesn't ask us to pray in specifics because He doesn't know what we want, but because He wants *us* to know what we want. This brings us to our next very important tip.

In light of God's "no" or "not yet," our specific, faith-filled prayer must include those important four words that come from the heart and lips of Christ: "Thy will be done" (Matt. 6:10; Mark 14:36). When prayed in faith, there is nothing weak or diminutive about this prayer. On the contrary, it is the most profound prayer of faith and the most important prayer we can pray.

Tip 2: Pray the Deepest Prayer of Faith

I like to be in control of things. My wife likes to be in control of things. My four children like to be in control of things. Being in control is one of the great idolatries of our age. If you disagree with this, pray, "Thy will be done" and mean it. It is very hard. Why? Because we like to be in control. (Herein lies the importance of inviting the Holy Spirit into your prayer. If you like to be in power, then be in the Holy Spirit—the power of God.)

Unleashing the Power of Intercessory Prayer

In praying the words "Thy will be done," we have a refined version of what detailed intercessory prayer ought to look like. It is prayer imbued with trust — the act of faith that is necessary for good prayer — and it states specifically: "I place You, God, as my number one!" At that moment, we say to God, "You know what my brother or sister in Christ needs before I ask, and I desire to enter into what You already know" (see Matt. 6:8). In praying this, we allow the holiness of God to make our imperfect intercessory prayers whole and holy (and thus part of our wholehearted prayer).

The prayer "Thy will be done" implies that there is a greater will than our own. It concedes that we do not know the divine plan of God. Therefore, even in our intercessions, we ought to knowingly place God's will before our own. All intercessory prayer needs to be open to the One who is the optimal Good because, while our prayers ask for a good, we must allow God to transform it into an even greater good — the greatest good — union with the Father. In some cases, we are asked to pray for the temporal healing of a loved one, such as healing from cancer, and we do so following the keys and tips laid out in this book. Still, as we do, we also pray for the calming of fear, and the like, that results from a conversion of heart, for it is the conversion of heart that leads to greater union with God the Father. Underneath every petition should be the intention to pray for the conversion of heart — for this is always the more excellent prayer.

The priority of praying for conversion is highlighted in the previously discussed narrative with Elijah (see James 5:13–18). In verse 17, we read that Elijah "prayed fervently that it might not rain." In effect, Elijah approached the throne of God to allow suffering and hardship to afflict the people to convert them. Elijah believed this extreme measure was what they needed. And this upright prayer was answered with a crisis. Often, crises bring people to their knees and back to God. The word "crisis" is defined as "turning point; decisive point; or that which separates." When we pray for a soul in crisis, we do so in the hope that God will use the crisis as a definitive point of change, a turning point for the soul for whom we are praying. By far, the number-one request I have received for intercessory prayer is the prayer for the conversion of a loved one.

We ought to see that our specific, intercessory prayer, even for a fallen-away loved one, should never be reduced to a cry of distress. It should be animated as a faith-filled desire to see God reveal His infinite, beautiful design for the one for whom we are praying. You can pick any three colors of the rainbow, put them together, and it would be pleasing to your eyes, but to witness all seven colors come together is a different kind of beauty. God's will is a different kind of beauty (especially on the Cross), and this is what we await; this is what we pray for. In other words, our prayer for others should never be content with seeing only the colors of violet, indigo, and blue paint the sky — the partial beauty of the whole — but should look for violet, indigo, blue, green, yellow, orange, and red — the entire attraction. Read the life of any saint, and you will see the splendor of beauty in all its fullness!

To say, "Thy will be done" (and mean it) can be difficult — especially when we want a particular outcome. We have grown accustomed to having what we want instantly. From Uber to Doordash, the *I* is being served at an accelerating rate. We have iPads, iPhones, iPods, and iDrives to load our iTunes onto. We use selfie sticks to take selfies. Of the original batch of social media sites, MySpace was the most popular. We live in a world where everything around us is continually emphasizing the *I*, the *self*, the *my*, and the *me*. We have placed ourselves at the center of existence and have placed everything else around us accordingly.

When I place myself at the center of the cosmos, my prayer life becomes very "Joe-centric" as opposed to Christocentric.

Joe-centrism desires quick satisfaction and the easy road (even for the one for whom I am praying). When my prayer life is in Joe-centric mode, if I do not get the answer I want, I throw it back at God. The challenge before us is this: what wealth do we honor? If we choose divine wealth, we choose Christocentrism, which holds Christ at the center of all we do. Christocentrism desires the definitive good, which is often the more difficult path. To take a cue from Hans Urs von Balthasar's playbook,[46] we must overcome the ego-drama, which wants to produce and direct every move, to enter the Theo-drama. which is unconditionally open to God's storyline, to God's will. When Christ entered human history, He lived not for Himself but for others. His was the life that prayed, "Not as I will, but as thou wilt" (Matt. 26:39).

Praying, "Not as I want, but as You want" or "Not according to my finite thinking, but according to Your infinite wisdom" is the part we play in the drama of intercessory prayer. Once we acquire this Christ-centered disposition in our intercessory prayer, we will be led down the path of perseverance and consistency—"for God denies Himself to no one who perseveres."[47] This kind of intercessory prayer brings peace to the soul as we loosen our grasp on what we cannot control. In life, great windstorms will arise, and waves will beat down on us. We will be tempted to question whether Jesus cares (see Mark 4:38), *but* do we allow Christ to calm the storms in our lives with His words: "Peace, be still"

---

[46] The renowned theologian Hans Urs von Balthasar penned a five-volume work titled *Theo-Drama*, in which he reflects upon the universe as the stage with the God-Man as the central character. The five volumes are presented within the construct of drama (actor, playwright, director, and so forth) to expound upon the salvific work of Christ.

[47] Saint Teresa of Avila, *The Life of Saint Teresa of Avila by Herself* (London, England: Penguin Classics, 1957), 77.

(Mark 4:39)? Do we allow such peace to consume our intercessory prayer? Let the words of Saint Paul wash over us: "Have no anxiety about anything, but in everything by prayer and supplication with thanksgiving let your requests be made known to God. And the peace of God, which surpasses all understanding, will keep your hearts and minds in Christ Jesus" (Phil. 4:6–7). Intercessory prayer leads to greater peace and guards the heart against the wicked snares of the devil.

Essentially, the prayer "Thy will be done" teaches us that petitions of intercession offer to God the needs of our brothers and sisters in Christ with the confidence that God will act according to His merciful love — the optimal good. This confidence is aware that God will never take anything away from us because everything already belongs to Him — all is a gift! The First Letter of John reminds us as much: "And this is the confidence which we have in him, that if we ask anything according to his will, he hears us. And if we know that he hears us in whatever we ask, we know that we have obtained the requests made of him" (1 John 5:14–15).

If Jesus is in us by grace and faith, and we abide in Him, then the petitions we gather up and offer to Him are fused in His Spirit, and the Father hears us. If we are not in Jesus, we lack faith and will "ask *wrongly*" (see James 1:5–6; 4:1–3). If our prayer seeks only to gratify our selfish desires, God cannot say yes to that prayer, for He is absolute unselfishness. Again, all good prayer arises from union with God. What do we do if we *feel* we are praying *rightly*?

On the one hand, Jesus tells us to "ask, seek, and knock," which, again, is the persistent prayer that leads us to banging on God's door. But what if He still does not answer? We then interpret His silence as His answer. God's first language was silence, and this divine silence waits for us at the center of our being. Silence often proves itself to be God's clear word inviting us to go deeper into His mysterious, unknown will. God's silence can be His speaking loudly to the need for us to be wildly open to His infinite design. In our communication with others, we sometimes realize that what we thought was good was not ideal. The same thing happens with God.

As we take our prayers to our all-knowing God, His return on our investment of prayer is exponential — exponential in its beauty — a return that includes the brilliance of the violet, indigo, and blue, in light of the green, orange, yellow, and red.

The story is told of Alexander the Great that one day, upon heading home from a victorious battle, his caravan came upon a beggar who asked for a copper coin. Initially, the courtier sent him away, but King Alexander intervened and asked what the poor man wanted. The courtier answered. The king then looked at the beggar and gave him an entire bag of gold coins. The courtier was surprised by this gift and commented, "Sir, a copper coin would have adequately met the beggar's need and desire. Why give him gold?" Alexander responded as a king responds, "A copper coin would suit the beggar's need, but gold coins suit Alexander's giving."

So often, we go to God in our intercessory prayer asking for one thing, and God desires to give us so much more. For us to receive this "more" that God wants to give, sometimes He responds with a "no" or "not yet." When God answers our prayer with a "no" or "not yet," we ought to hear, "I have something better in mind" — for behind every "no" or "not yet" is an immeasurably greater "yes" — the "yes" to the salvation of souls.

We often say hindsight is 20/20: "If only I knew, I would not have acted in that way." Well, accepting God's "no" or "not yet" as an answer to our petitions of intercession is faith's 20/20. God's "no" and "not yet" help us to avoid "acting in that way." God is a Father who is always looking out for the "best interests" of His children — including and especially the one for whom we are praying. Parents are always on the lookout for their child's best interests long term, which means saying "no" and "not yet" from time to time. Think of how much hope we should glean from the Father's "no," recognizing that it is an exercise of the greatness of His love and will lead to something better! Just as we need to be in relationship with our parents to understand the reasons behind their "no," all the more do we need to be in relationship with our heavenly Father to better understand the reasons behind His "no" to our petitions of intercession. We do this through the reading of Scripture, the wisdom of the saints, and increasing our conversations with God in personal prayer.

The Son of God left this world with a crown, but a crown that very few understood. It was the crown given to a King who shows us how to fight the good fight, keep the faith, persevere in the race, and finish the course (see 2 Tim. 4:7 and Heb. 12:1). Our crucified King has revealed to us that doing the Father's will is not the road most traveled, but the road "less traveled." If we are going to share in this great mystery of doing the Father's will and lead others down this path, we must seek out the deeper wisdom that lies behind the "no." This deeper wisdom is the confident assurance that by accepting God's "no," we are saying "yes" to the riches of God that far exceed the value of any gold coin because they belong not to any kingdom of this world but to the everlasting Kingdom.[48] These riches consist in the actual sharing of God's very life and the treasures His grace provides. God's delay to answer us is not denial or rejection; it is the action necessary to bringing about a more magnificent "yes" that will, through our cooperation with His grace, lead us to heaven.

Prayer is about union with Jesus through a union of hearts, a union of wants. From this union of wants, the soul prays freely:

---

[48] For more reflection on King Alexander and a king's riches, see Joseph Hollcraft, "A King's Riches," SpiritualDirection.com, August 18, 2015, https://spiritualdirection.com/2015/08/18/a-kings-riches.

Unleashing the Power of Intercessory Prayer

"Thy will be done." To desire what Jesus desires is to order every other desire. We must have confidence in this truth as we pray for others because it will help bring resolution to the soul for whom we are praying. So, let us be sure to include in our intercessory prayer those four words, "Thy will be done," when we look to better respond to the request: "Will you pray for me?"

Tip 3: Keep a List of Your Intentions and Create a Sacred Space

Growing up, I was very disheveled and unorganized. Consequently, when I went off to college and needed to keep a tight schedule, I failed miserably. My first semester of college went poorly because I failed to keep a schedule. With the help of my first roommate, who is the most punctual and detailed person I have ever met, I quickly learned that if I was going to succeed, I needed to write things down, put them into a schedule, and follow through. When I began to write things down, I was better able to achieve my goals.

Praying for others is a very practical thing. The simple act of writing down the names and intentions in a notebook (or in your phone) is an important practical step. Sometimes I get so many requests that I won't remember all of them unless I write them down. You may better remember the requests if you prayed for those intentions on the spot, but it is still important to write them down to follow up later with more prayer. This leads us to the importance of creating a sacred space for prayer.

Where might we go to set up a sacred space for prayer? Jesus says, "When you pray, go into your room and shut the door and pray to your Father who is in secret; and your Father who sees in secret will reward you" (Matt. 6:6). Jesus sends us to our rooms, and He does so for disciplinary reasons—the discipline of better prayer. The quiet of our rooms is a good place for a sacred space.

In our rooms, we should set up a table with a crucifix as our focal point. On that table, we ought to place statues and prayer cards of the saints as reminders that we belong to a God who encourages intercession. Also, on the altar we have created, we should light a candle for our petitions. Hanging a crucifix over our prayer space allows us to lay the petitions at the feet of Christ (and there is no better place for petitions to go). There, invoke the presence of the Holy Spirit, dig deep from the heart with sighs and groans, and pray with fervor for the petitions you have laid at the foot of the Cross.

If you are fortunate enough to have a perpetual adoration chapel in your local parish, go there as often as possible. There is no better "sacred space" than the space where God is present. Adoration of the Blessed Sacrament is the space of intimacy and silence where intercessory prayer is most vibrant. "Draw near to God and He will draw near to you" (James 4:8).

Regarding this topic to keep intentions and to find a sacred space to pray, I often receive the question: "How long should I pray for the intention I received?" Simply put—that is up to God! In practice, we ought to hold on to the names and circumstances we pray for until the prayer is answered. In some cases, we may be praying for a specific intention until our last waking breaths. Personally, there are petitions for conversion that I have been praying for ... for a very long time. In the end, we ought to concern ourselves less with the *quantity* of time we are praying for an intention and give more attention to the *quality* of time we are spending in prayer. God will take care of the rest!

The goal of intercessory prayer is to intercede for the one who has asked for our prayers. In the simple steps of writing down the petitions entrusted to us and creating sacred space for prayer, we take two necessary steps in following through on our promises to pray for those we care about.

Unleashing the Power of Intercessory Prayer

Key Patron: Venerable Cardinal Van Thuan

Cardinal Francis Xavier Nguyen Van Thuan was the nephew of an assassinated president, a prisoner of the communist regime in Vietnam, and a priest and bishop of the Catholic Church. By the time of his death, he was beloved by millions within and outside his home country of Vietnam for his heroic witness to hope. He is currently recognized as Venerable Cardinal Van Thuan.

Born in Vietnam in 1928, young Francis Van Thuan entered the seminary at the age of thirteen and was ordained twelve years later on June 11, 1953. Father Van Thuan quickly rose in popularity and become a bishop in the Diocese of Nha Trang in 1967 during the Vietnam War. Eight years later, he was appointed Archbishop of Saigon, just two days before Saigon fell to North Vietnam. Soon thereafter, on August 15, 1975, Archbishop Van Thuan was arrested by the authorities and imprisoned for thirteen years, nine of them in solitary confinement. In the darkness of his prison cell in Hanoi, North Vietnam, he was purged of self-centeredness, and the heart of a saintly man was forged. It wasn't until November 21, 1988, that Archbishop Van Thuan was released from prison.[49]

In his first weeks in prison, Archbishop Van Thuan struggled to come to grips with the misfortunes that had beset him. One night, as he sought the Lord's counsel, he heard Him speak from the depths of his heart.

> Alone in my prison cell, I continued to be tormented by the fact that I was forty-eight years old, in the prime of my life, that I had worked for eight years as a bishop and gained so

---

[49] Cardinal Van Thuan entered prison on the Marian solemnity of the Assumption (August 15) and left on the Marian feast of the Presentation of the Blessed Virgin Mary (November 21). This ought to be considered a sign the Mother of God was personally accompanying the Vietnamese cardinal in his Dark Night of the Soul.

much pastoral experience and there I was isolated, inactive and far from my people.

One night, from the depths of my heart I could hear a voice advising me: "Why torment yourself? You must discern between God and the works of God—everything you have done and desire to continue to do, pastoral visits, training seminarians, sisters and members of religious orders, building schools, and evangelizing non-Christians. All of that is excellent work, the work of God, but it is not God! If God wants you to give it all up and put the work into his hands, do it and trust him. God will do the work infinitely better than you; he will entrust the work to others who are more able than you. You have only to choose God and not the works of God!"[50]

Archbishop Van Thuan would begin to enter the mystery of God's plan, recognizing his misfortune as fortunate for his salvation (for what is misfortune is often fortunate to our salvation), but it took time. Gradually, over those thirteen years, his prison cells were transformed into sanctuaries of hope.

Two months after the archbishop was sent to prison, a seven-year-old boy by the name of Quang smuggled paper into his prison cell. Archbishop Van Thuan began to jot down Scripture passages he had memorized (up to three hundred of them) and his reflections upon them. Those pages eventually became books with hope as their central theme.

The authorities were aware of Archbishop Van Thuan's goodness, and they feared that the guards might convert to the Catholic

[50] Extracts from "Experiencing God's Liberating Power," a talk Cardinal Van Thuan gave at a religious education congress in Los Angeles in 2002, shortly before passing away. "How Faith Survived in a Communist Prison," Cardinal Nguyen Van Thuan Foundation, http://www.card-fxthuan.org/his-works/faith-survived-in-prison.php.

Faith. Therefore, they regularly changed the cadre of security guards. It did not work. Van Thuan's encounters with the guards were leading to conversions, and in some cases, the prison guards could be heard singing the Salve Regina and the Veni Creator.

After Van Thuan was released, Pope John Paul II appointed him head of the Pontifical Council for Peace, elevating him to cardinal in 2001. In that time, he preached to the Roman Curia, and his spiritual conferences were published. Cardinal Van Thuan's trilogy on hope — *The Road to Hope, The Prayers of Hope*, and *Testimony of Hope* — continues to encourage people today. Cardinal Van Thuan died of a rare form of cancer on September 16, 2002.

Like the saints previously discussed, Venerable Cardinal Francis Xavier Nguyen Van Thuan radiated light in a place of profound darkness, bringing souls to Christ every step of the way. He was a signpost of love, interceding for everyone in his path.

We invoke the intercession of Van Thuan in this key of praying with specifics because in this chapter we engaged the most powerful prayer of all: "Thy will be done." Among the many words of wisdom of Venerable Van Thuan stands the overarching truth that hope begins when doubt ends. You must stop tormenting yourself with doubt and accept the present moment for what it is — a gift from God that He desires to use for your salvation and the salvation of others.

Archbishop Van Thuan knew how to pray the great four-word prayer because he first *genuinely* asked the very human two-word prayer, "Why me?" Archbishop Van Thuan had been a canonist who wanted to catechize the people of Vietnam, desiring their renewal through a deepening of faith; yet, he found himself imprisoned. So, unable to carry out his catechesis, he questioned God, "Why me?" And as he *genuinely* asked, he *genuinely* listened, learning to pray with great affection, "Thy will be done." In fact, by praying the seven petitions of the Our Father, including "thy will be done," he acquired a deep intimacy with and greater love for God. His prayer became very personal. In the silence of his cell, in the calm of his heart, he prayed, and he listened. He may have been in solitary confinement for nine years, but was he ever *really* alone? No. God was always with him.

Our last tip emphasized the importance of writing down prayer requests. Imagine the poverty we would all have if the good archbishop never wrote down his inspirations. We ought to be encouraged to write down not only the names of those for whom we pray but also the thoughts that God is inspiring us to reflect upon — these thoughts might take the form of insights to share with those for whom we are praying.

Venerable Van Thuan often asked his friends to send him what he called his "medicine." His "medicine" was cough-syrup bottles filled with wine and small fragments of bread. The beloved archbishop was then able to celebrate Mass every day at 3:00 p.m., the hour of mercy. He would use his palm as his altar.

Venerable Cardinal Francis Xavier Nguyen Van Thuan was very personal in his prayer, learning the language of praying, "Thy will be done," and encouraging us, by way of example, to be practical in our prayer lives and write down the stirrings of our hearts.

Venerable Cardinal Francis Xavier Nguyen Van Thuan, pray for us!

Prompt Questions for Journaling

1. Do we pray to God personally, intentionally, and with specifics? Reflect.
2. Do you have a physical prayer space at home where you can pray your petitions of intercession?

7

Pray in Friendship with Christ

In the summer of 2008, while studying at Oxford University, I had the blessed opportunity to dine with a priest friend of mine, Father Walter, at The Eagle and Child Pub.[51] Throughout our conversation, we were led to reflect upon the two men who made the Pub renowned: C.S. Lewis and J.R.R. Tolkien.

Father Walter and I talked about many things that cool summer evening in Oxford: Lewis and Tolkien's initial days together in Oxford, where they bonded over discussions on Norse mythology; Tolkien's role in bringing C.S. Lewis into Christianity; and their mutual critique of each other's work. As we discussed the deep bond between the two, we also reflected upon their more turbulent days as they grew older, when their opinions of each other's work became more and more callous. In one case, Tolkien writes, "It is sad that 'Narnia' and all that part of C.S. Lewis's work should remain outside the range of my sympathy, as much of my work was outside his."[52]

---

[51] The Eagle and Child is famous for its association with the Inklings writers' group to which J.R.R. Tolkien and C.S. Lewis belonged.

[52] Humphrey Carpenter and Christopher Tolkien, *The Letters of J.R.R. Tolkien* (Boston: Houghton Mifflin Harcourt, 2000), letter 532.

Whatever discontent there was between the two literary giants, the bond of their friendship transcended time. Just a few days after Lewis's death, Tolkien wrote to his daughter, "So far I have felt the normal feelings of a man of my age — like an old tree that is losing all its leaves one by one: This feels like an ax-blow near the roots. Very sad that we should have been so separated in the last years; but our time of close communion endured in memory for both of us."[53] After bringing this line from Tolkien's memoirs into our discussion, Father Walter then observed, "I suppose we could say the true measure of one's friendship is how hard we feel that blow." Real friendships have deep roots!

Intercessory Key: Pray in Friendship with Christ

Saint Teresa of Avila once said that "prayer is nothing more than being on terms of friendship with God." If real relationships have deep roots, then we want our friendship with God to have the deepest roots.

We read in the Gospel of John, "No longer do I call you servants ... but I have called you friends, for all that I have heard from my Father I have made known to you" (John 15:15). During His farewell discourse on the night of His arrest, Jesus called His disciples friends because He had "made known" everything to them. The God-Man was approaching His death, and He let *man* know what is nearest to the heart of God — friendship with Him!

We talk with our friends, laugh with our friends, dine with our friends. We tell our closest friends everything. In this seventh key, Saint Teresa of Avila counsels us to pay close attention to God, hang out with Jesus, and talk with Him. Hold nothing back, turn over everything to Him.

[53] Ibid., Letter 251.

Just after calling His disciples friends, Jesus declares, "You did not choose me, but I chose you that you should go and bear fruit and that your fruit should abide; so that whatever you ask the Father in my name, he may give it to you" (John 15:16).[54] If our petitions of intercession are offered to God in His name, He will grant us our hearts' desires. Calling Jesus friend is indispensable to our intercessory prayer because in the closeness and intimacy of friendship, the listen-response attentiveness is at its best. Jesus speaks; we listen. We speak; Jesus listens. Therefore, get close to Him—call Jesus friend!

Tip 1: Call Jesus Friend

What does it mean to call someone a friend? A friend is a person with whom you share your heart and who shares his heart with you. Friendship builds upon vulnerability, the willingness to open our hearts to those we trust. We confide in friends who will look out for our best interests and respond accordingly. The deeper a friendship goes in willingness, vulnerability, and personal entrustment, the more pronounced its growth. As we spend time with our friends, we pick up each other's habits—good and bad. As friendship grows, we begin to see ourselves in the other. The places we like to go, the programs we watch, the music we listen to, the games and sports we play, the people we get along with—everything that makes up the time we spend together unites us. Our friend becomes like a mirror in which we see ourselves.

There are friends, and then there is our best friend. Your best friend knows everything about you. They know the good, the bad, and the ugly, and they know when you are feeling good, bad, or

---

[54] In this passage, the "may" implies the prayer of right intention, which is swept up in the optimal good previously mentioned.

ugly. (At least my wife, who is my best friend, does.) They know what makes us tick and what ticks us off. Our best friends are the best reflections we have of ourselves because they contain all the secrets that we would not share with anyone else.

We call Jesus friend because we believe that He wants what is best for us. We confide in Him because we trust Him. But what is "mind numbing" about this call to be friends with Jesus is that He desires to be not just our friend but our best friend, or in the words of my five-year-old, "our bestest friend" (because bestest is better than best).

In the Gospel, Jesus asked His Apostles: "Who do you say that I am?" (Matt. 16:15). Jesus wants to know what His friends think about Him, not for His sake, but for ours. Jesus did not need a self-esteem boost; rather, He was providing an opportunity for the disciples to personalize their relationship with Him. It was then that Peter stepped forward and said, "You are the Christ, the Son of the living God" (Matt. 16:16). Just as the disciples were invited to identify who Christ was in their lives, so are we. Fundamentally, as Christians, we must ask the question: Who is Jesus to me? Do I call Him friend?

In the introduction, I touched upon the full vision of our anthropology, composite body and soul. As we pray our devotions, receive Christ in the sacramental life, read Scripture fervently, study the lives of the saints, and serve the poor, the depth of our friendship with Christ will grow and so will our understandings of who we are as human persons. In studying Christ, we will better understand not only the functional part of what we do but also the more meaningful part of who we are in our relationships with God—that which animates what we do. The more we get to know Him, the more we get to know ourselves. Jesus is not just any friend, but the One Friend who reveals to us how to be a better human being, the best friend we could ever hope for.

We must pay attention to Christ's "revealing" Himself to us, both in divine revelation and in the more informal revelation we find in our everyday conversation with Him. This "paying attention" happens in proximity and silence.

Tip 2: Pray in Proximity and Silence

Friendship prayer calls for the prayer of proximity. Our intercessory prayer is at its best when we draw near to God in silence. We draw near to Him physically when we visit the Blessed Sacrament; we draw near to Him mystically when we contemplate the Spirit's clandestine movements in our hearts. Friendships grow when friends communicate in proximity. When my friend calls me and needs to talk, if I am able, I hang up the phone and go to him. Why? Because closeness allows for a different kind of communication. It offers more than just words; it involves facial expressions, feelings, and body language.

By proximity to Jesus as friend, we pray better, listen better, understand better, and respond better. The closer we are to Jesus, the more in tune with Him we become. Recall what I said in the introduction on prayer, that our *obedient* response to Christ is one that is "in tune" (*ob-audire*) and that our behavior is *absurd* when we are "out of tune" (*absurdis*). To pray for others on terms of friendship with Christ is to pray close to Him, and in that closeness, He teaches us how to pray closely with those who have asked for our prayer.

In chapter 5, we talked about the importance of praying on the spot — a point that has more weight once we consider the value of praying closely with others. Dan Burke's intercessory prayer moved me because of his willingness to pray on the spot, but also because I was near to Him. When we walk in the presence of God, we carry within us a presence that can be a source of consolation to others when we pray with them in proximity. Practically speaking, the most surefire intercessory prayer is praying with our friend before the Blessed Sacrament—this is proximate prayer, par excellence!

Friendship prayer that is proximate also calls for silence. When are you most silent? (Pause and ask yourself this question honestly.) I am most silent when I am listening to my favorite songs and watching my favorite movies and plays. In other words, I am most silent when I am a captive audience—when I desire to behold someone or something. Silence is synonymous with beholding. The word "behold" can be found 1,298 times in the Bible. The best translation of this word might be something like "Pay close attention to what I am about to say; it is very important!" Just as I pay close attention to the Piano Guys and Russell Crowe in *Gladiator*, so I should pay close attention to what God is saying to me (even more so, in fact).

Silence is virtuous when we have something to say but choose to remain in the interior school of waiting—the classroom where attentive listening teaches us when to say what, if anything. In our prayer life, to listen is to be held captive by the One speaking, instructing us on the revelation He wants us to behold. The more we go to Jesus as a friend and attentively listen to the Word of God, the more acutely we will hear His still, soft voice. Respond to the question "Will you pray for me?" with a heart captive for Jesus Christ!

The call for silent, proximate prayer in friendship with Christ echoes our treatment on contemplative prayer because "contemplative prayer [*oración mental*] ... is nothing else than a close sharing between friends; it means taking time frequently to be alone with him who we know loves us."[55]

---

[55] St. Teresa of Jesus, *The Book of Her Life*, 8, 5, in *The Collected Works of St. Teresa of Avila*, vol. 1, trans. Kieran Kavanaugh, O.C.D., and O. Rodriguez, O.C.D. (Washington DC: Institute of Carmelite Studies, 1976), 67. Also, see CCC 2709.

Perhaps most commonly, our loved ones ask us to pray for intentions of great importance: a significant decision they need to make, an exam that will impact their future, a friend who has left the Faith, a job interview, cancer victims, or a prayer to meet their future spouse. All these prayer requests define one's life; they are the crossroad moments — the conflicts that lead to either victory or defeat. As discussed in chapter 6, our intercessory prayer has the foremost purpose of offering to God the needs of our brothers and sisters in Christ with the confidence that God will act according to His merciful, optimal good.

Tip 3: Pray with Fasting

As we probe the importance of friendship prayer, we ought to consider the context that Jesus first called His disciples "friends" (John 15:15). From the Cross, our friend Jesus says to us, "This is how much I love you!" Love is physical; to sacrifice one's body is to express physically the words, "I love you!" If sighs and groans are the love language of the Holy Spirit, then suffering is Christ's love language.

The Cross is the high point of intercessory prayer. From the actual point where the horizontal and vertical beams *inter*sect, the God-Man prays, *inter*cedes, uniting heaven and earth, uniting God the Father with man's petitions. In order to bring about these petitions and open the gates of heaven, Christ offered Himself as a lamb led to the slaughter for the ransom of man. We read in the letter to the Hebrews 5:7–10:

> Jesus offered up prayers and supplications, with loud cries and tears, to the one who was able to save him from death, and he was heard because of his reverent submission. Although he was a Son, he learned obedience through what he suffered; and having been made perfect, he became the

source of eternal salvation for all who obey him, having been designated by God a high priest according to the order of Melchizedek.[56]

From our crosses, when we pray, we unite our horizontal existences with the vertical, bringing down the presence of God into the people for whom we pray and the circumstances that need His healing presence and transforming love. In what way can we be intentional in our sacrificial intercessions? How might our prayers of intercession be physical? How can we enter into Christ's most powerful love language? By fasting.

Fasting is a humble, "interior penance" (CCC 1434; see Matt. 6:16–18) in which a person willingly deprives the body of food, nourishment, and the enjoyment of taste. Fasting from what our bodies require, or merely crave, is a beautiful prayer and a powerful love language that we ought to bring into our intercessory prayer. The primitive root of the Hebrew word for "fasting," *tsom*, is *tsuwm*, which translates as "to cover over (as the mouth)." When fasting, we ought always to be mindful of covering our mouth from food. In the words of Tobit, "Prayer is good when accompanied by fasting, almsgiving, and righteousness" (Tob. 12:8). Essentially, fasting carries out Paul's exhortation to present our "bodies as a living sacrifice, holy and acceptable to God, which is our spiritual worship" (Rom. 12:1). In this sense, fasting proves itself as a deeply holy act.

Christ's death on the Cross is a manifestation of the divine, selfless love shared between the Father and the Son. Following the example of Christ's ultimate sacrifice, the moment we receive any gift from the Holy Spirit is the moment we are called to give it away in selfless love, and the moment we give it away in selfless love is

---

[56] The Greek word for "offering" in this text also translates as "sacrifice," showing that offering and sacrifice belong together.

the moment we receive more of God's love. This divine logic of love is the great paradox of our Faith. You want more love, then give more away in sacrificial acts. The Christian life is a continual lesson in the "mathematics of God," where subtraction equals addition, loss equals profit, and death equals life. Even when we ourselves are down to nothing, or when our petitions seem hopeless, God's miraculous "mathematics" can make something beautiful come from nothing. God makes holy what we give Him, and when we give Him a sacrifice, such as a fast, it makes more holy our prayer of intercession (the Latin *sacrum fice* translates as "to make holy").

As already touched upon, traditionally, we define love as willing the good of others for their own sakes, without the expectation of receiving anything in return. In the words of Karol Wojtyla (Pope Saint John Paul II), "Love consists of a commitment which limits one's freedom — it is a giving of the self, and to give oneself means just that: to limit one's freedom on behalf of another."[57] Freedom is not a license to do whatever we want to do, but the power, in reason and will, to choose what we ought to do. Freedom is to be in possession of oneself. Here again, what is contrary to expectation is what is true: to gain freedom, one must limit one's freedom.

"Love" is an action verb that describes what one feels for another and, at times, what words struggle to convey. The deeper our love for Christ, the greater we define love with the action of sacrifice. In intercessory prayer, fasting is a profound expression of love. When we go to God by subtracting something from our routines (fasting), God will add something to the life of the one for whom we are praying. Again, this is how God's arithmetic works in the Body of Christ. God can always be found in the space created by the emptying of our selfish wants and desires.

---

[57] Karol Wojtyla, *Love and Responsibility* (San Francisco: Ignatius Press, 1993), 135.

Unleashing the Power of Intercessory Prayer

We fast because it changes things. The Ninevites repented of their evil ways with a forty-day fast, and what did God do? He spared them. "When God saw what they did, how they turned from their evil way, God repented of the evil which he had said he would do to them; and he did not do it" (Jon 3:10). *Fasting changes things.*

In the famous story of Queen Esther, we have another example of the power of fasting. In the story, King Ahasuerus sent out a proclamation declaring a set day for the execution of all the Jews in the kingdom because one of them, Mordecai, had refused to pay homage to him. Mordecai then sought out Queen Esther, a Jew herself, to go to the king and intercede on behalf of the Jewish people. She agreed but first urged Mordecai to have all the Jews fast for three days and three nights (see Esther 4:16). Esther was not going to go before the king without the interceding power of fasting. The fast worked, as King Ahasuerus lifted the edict and granted mercy upon Mordecai and the Jewish people. *Fasting changes things.*

In the New Testament, after Christ expelled from a boy a demon whom the disciples were unable to exorcise, they inquire, "Why could we not cast it out?" Christ's response is telling: "This kind can come out only by prayer and fasting" (Matt. 17:19, 21). So, although Christ gave the apostles power to remove unclean spirits (see Mark 6:7), they were unable to remove *this* unclean spirit. If you read this story in the Gospel of Mark, "this kind" of demon was particularly volatile, casting the boy "into the fire and into the water, to destroy him" (9:22). If we receive a request that we find particularly difficult, then that's the kind of intercessory prayer that needs fasting. Why? Because *fasting changes things*, even supposedly insurmountable things.

On one occasion, a penitent approached Father John Vianney and asked him why his constant intercessory prayer for the conversion of a loved one was not bearing fruit. He responded: "But have you fasted?"

Christ's words, "This kind can come out only by prayer and fasting," raise another point. We should be aware of the spiritual warfare that manifests itself in intercessory prayer. Well-intentioned intercessory prayer seeks change for the better. Satan does not want this. Herein lies the battle: change for the better versus ongoing complacency of the soul—this calls for fervent prayer that is persevering when resolution is not immediate. *Persevering fasting changes things!*

Ultimately, fasting as a practice is at its best when the Holy Spirit leads us. Only then can it be an offering of "reverent submission" (Heb. 5:7)—for reverence is a fruit of the Holy Spirit. In the opening chapter of this book, we underscored the life of intercessory prayer as a life in the Holy Spirit. Our fasting will bear its greatest fruit when we draw our strength from the Holy Spirit. Again, the Holy Spirit is the protagonist of our nudging, prompting, and inspiration. Jesus was led "full of the Holy Spirit" into the desert (Luke 4:1). The person who is "led" does not push away from, resist, or turn his back on the One leading, but receives, listens to, and walks toward Him. Just as the Holy Spirit led and inspired Jesus to fast in the desert, so, too, does He lead and inspire us to fast for those who have asked for our prayers.[58]

As you draw near to God as His friend, allow Him to show you what it means to be a friend. God might invite you to fast for your friend and the petition you hold in your heart.

Key Patron: Saint Teresa of Avila

The saints lived their whole converted lives as friends of Christ. So how does one begin to ascertain what saint is most appropriate to

---

[58] We can also say that fasting is a form of "journeying with" that gains spiritual wealth for the suffering person. At the same time, "journeying with" the suffering person helps you to know him better, which can help with adding specifics to the intercessory prayer.

turn to as an intercessor for this key of praying in friendship with God? By turning to the woman who significantly helped shape our understanding of what it means to pray in close proximity to God, Saint Teresa of Avila.

The childhood of Teresa of Avila was not atypical of girls her age during the sixteenth century (1515–1582). While she had pious tendencies, she enjoyed boys and materialism as much as the next girl. At times in her adolescence, she would read inappropriate books with unsavory images and words. While the reading of profane books was a point of distraction for young Teresa, her schooling with the Augustinian nuns and her practice of spiritual reading gradually opened her eyes. Her spiritual formation led her to a place of recollection and contemplation of holy things.

There was a war being raged within her soul — one that would come to a crescendo after she became a religious. At the age of sixteen, to the chagrin of her father, she entered the convent of the Incarnation in Avila. At the age of twenty, she professed solemn vows to the Carmelite way of life. For approximately the next twenty years, Sister Teresa would struggle with an inconsistent prayer life. Initially, after a health scare that had her in a coma for four days, she found the repose of religious life consoling and grew deeper in mental and contemplative prayer. However, in time, her prayer life stalled and she fell again into inconsistency and stagnancy. It was not until Lent, when she was thirty-nine, that everything would change.

On a Friday evening, walking up the church steps to pray the Liturgy of the Hours, she encountered a statue of the Holy Face of Christ crucified (*Ecce Homo*). Upon looking at the wounded Face, she was pierced to the heart. Teresa fell to the ground and told Jesus that she would not get up until she had received the grace necessary never to backslide in prayer again. She wept unceasingly and was never the same.

After this encounter with God, she understood more deeply the call to be unceasing in prayer. In the words of the saint, not to pray was like "a baby turning from its mother's breasts, what can be expected but death?"[59]

In Saint Teresa's vision of prayer, she saw the heart as an enclosed garden into which the soul invites Jesus as a true friend. The more we pray to Jesus as an intimate friend, the more we water the garden of our hearts. However, for water to reach the garden, it needs to be pumped in. The prayer of *silence*, for Saint Teresa, was the pump to the garden. Just as the pump makes it possible for liquid to reach its destination point, so, too, silence makes it possible for God's voice to reach our hearts. Saint Teresa envisioned silence as quintessential to transforming the garden of our hearts into a cascade of blooms.

Saint Teresa of Avila would spend at least one hour a day in silence. Sixty minutes of no noise. Think about that. Saint Teresa of Avila's heart was in full bloom because of the prayer of silence.

What does this mean for our intercessory prayer? The deeper we go in the spiritual life, the greater the bloom; the greater the bloom, the stronger the scent of intercession. Indeed, God smiles favorably upon the upward movement of a strong, pleasing aroma (see Gen. 8:20–22). Toward the end of Saint Teresa's autobiography, we read that Jesus promised to bestow favors upon those for whom she prayed.[60] Indeed, the prayer of Saint Teresa of Avila was filled with a strong, pleasing aroma—and what is the strong aroma, if not fasting—*the strongest* aroma in intercessory prayer!

As discussed in our third tip, the power of fasting is a power that can move mountains. Saint Teresa was very strong on this point.

---

[59] "St. Teresa of Avila," Catholic Online, https://www.catholic.org/saints/saint.php?saint_id=208.

[60] *The Life of Saint Teresa of Avila by herself*, 295–305.

She tells us that the devil does not want us to fast, even causing us to fear it. She writes, "Our human nature often asks for more than what it needs, and sometimes the devil helps so as to cause fear about the practice of penance and fasting."[61] Elsewhere, she counsels us to be encouraged by the One we call friend: "Whoever lives in the presence of so good a friend and excellent a leader, who went ahead of us to be the first to suffer, can endure all things. The Lord helps us, strengthens us, and never fails; He is a true friend."[62] Indeed, Saint Teresa did not live in fear of fasting as she would fast up to eight months out of the year.

Interestingly, we opened up discussion of this key with the words of Saint Teresa of Avila, "Prayer is nothing more than being on terms of friends with God." Because of this true friendship, she was able to embrace the call to be a "holy and acceptable offering to God" (Rom. 12:1) through constant prayer and fasting. We ought to pray to her for help as we set out to follow her example.

Saint Teresa of Avila, pray for us!

Prompt Questions for Journaling

1. Do you pray for your friend as a friend to Jesus? Reflect.
2. When are you most silent? Reflect.
3. What has been your experience with fasting? Do you allow yourself to be led by the Holy Spirit?

---

[61] Saint Teresa of Avila. *The Collected Works of Saint Teresa of Avila*, vol. 3, trans. Kieran Kavanaugh, O.C.D., and Otilio Rodrigues, O.C.D. (Washington DC: ICS Publications, 1985), 326.

[62] Saint Teresa of Avila. *The Collected Works of Saint Teresa of Avila*, vol. 1, 2nd ed., trans. Kieran Kavanaugh, O.C.D., and Otilio Rodrigues, O.C.D. (Washington DC: ICS Publications, 1987), 193.

8

Pray in Thanksgiving and Praise to God

According to a Jewish legend, after God created the world, He turned to the angels and asked what they thought of His work. "One of them replied that the world is so vast and so perfect that there was nothing wanting, except a voice to offer God that which is owed him, an expression of gratitude."[63]

Intercessory Key: Pray in Thanksgiving and Praise to God

To pray in thanksgiving to God is to express gratitude for the immensity of His revelation—natural and divine—by "continually offering up sacrifices of praise to God, that is, the fruit of lips that acknowledge his name" (Heb. 13:15). We pray this way in "all circumstances, for this is the will of God in Christ Jesus for you" (1 Thess. 5:18; see Eph. 5:20).

The more we pay attention to God, the more we will praise His name with our lips in all circumstances. God is continually moving in our lives and revealing Himself to us. His gifts are all around us. Do we see Him? Do we thank Him? The Mass is the sacrament

---

[63] Donald DeMarco, *The Heart of Virtue: Lessons from Life and Literature Illustrating the Beauty and Value of Moral Character* (San Francisco: Ignatius Press, 1996), 95.

of thanksgiving and our opportunity to offer Him gratitude for all the generous gifts He has bestowed on us.

Tip 1: Take your Petitions of Intercession with You to Mass

When the Hollcraft family goes on a special trip, we pack based on our anticipated needs. If it is a family vacation to Lake Tahoe, we will be sure to bring hiking boots, sunscreen, and swimsuits. If we are going to visit family in Ohio during Christmastime, we will be sure to bring heavy coats, mittens, and snow gear. Likewise, when we go to Mass each Sunday, we bring the petitions of intercession that have been entrusted to us. And as I teach my kids, we bring those requests to our worship and "place" them on the altar with the confidence and trust that God will answer our prayer (see Heb. 10:19–25).

In his 1947 encyclical *Mediator Dei* (The Mediator of God), Pope Pius XII reinforces the role of the laity in offering themselves to God in union with Jesus Christ. In this document, which places the highest priority on sharing in the one mediation of Christ, we ought to see our "conscious and active" involvement of sense and heart during Mass (how we "pay attention to God" in the Liturgy) as typical to the vocation of intercessory prayer.

The chief means of the "continual offering up sacrifices of praise" is the Eucharist — the prayer of "giving thanks" (*eucharistesas*). This prayer of thanksgiving to God is the salvific prayer of eternal intercession: Jesus "is able for all time to save those who draw near to God through Him, since he always lives to make intercession for them" (Heb. 7:25; see 1 Tim. 2:1–6). There is great power in placing our petitions on the altar as part of our offering of thanksgiving to God. It is especially fruitful to pray our petitions *into* the Eucharistic prayer of *epiclesis* — the prayer of invocation of the Holy Spirit upon the bread and wine in the Liturgy. As the Holy Spirit transforms the bread and wine on the altar into the Body, Blood, Soul, and Divinity of Jesus

Christ, we ought to pray that the Holy Spirit transforms the person or situation we have placed on the altar. For example, when we hear the words, "Make holy these gifts, we pray, by sending down your Spirit upon them like the dewfall" (Eucharistic Prayer II), we should place on the altar, in mind and heart, the petitions of intercession with which we have been entrusted. On the altar, excessive graces are available for the person or circumstance of our prayers. The altar is the table of grace, the physical place where the things of Heaven transform the things of Earth. Take all your petitions to the table of transformation and you will know the peace of God (see Phil 4:7)!

What's more, when the bread is "broken," so God breaks into the life of the broken soul for whom we are praying. As we place our intentions on the table of transformation, we ought to be prayerfully attentive to this invasion of grace.

God's intercessory graces also include the penitential prayer we say during the Penitential Rite and the Prayer of the Faithful. During the Penitential Rite, we pray: "I confess to almighty God and you, my brothers and sisters, that I have greatly sinned, in my thoughts and in my words, in what I have done and in what I have failed to do.... *Therefore I ask blessed Mary ever-Virgin, all the Angels and Saints, and you, my brothers and sisters, to pray for me to the Lord our God.*"[64] In this penitential prayer, there is a mutual request to pray for each other humbly. How often do we reflect on the importance of this moment, both as receiver and giver of a prayer request? Part of our "active participation" in Mass is to offer to God each soul who has just asked for our prayers.

During the Prayer of the Faithful, "the people respond in a certain way to the word of God which they have welcomed in faith

---

[64] United States Conference of Catholic Bishops (USCCB), *General Instruction of the Roman Missal* (Washington, DC: USCCB, 2003), 51, emphasis added.

and, exercising the office of their baptismal priesthood, offer prayers to God for the salvation of all."[65] So the petitions in the Prayer of the Faithful are an offering that is an exercise of our baptismal priesthood, otherwise known as our common priesthood (as opposed to the ministerial priesthood), whereby we share in the dying and rising of Christ. Once again, the mathematics of God are at play as we talk about our paradoxical faith; during Mass, we enter into the simultaneous dying and rising of Jesus on the altar.

Here again, while the scope of this book has been focused on responding to the question "Will you pray for me?" the Church always has in her prayers "for all." Recall, the Church exists for prayer, and she does this par excellence in the Eucharist. As the Prayer of the Faithful is offered to God, we unite ourselves to the Eucharistic sacrifice and the Mystical Body of Christ, to bring about the unseen, mysterious, grace-filled movements of God that effect transformation in the areas that need change — for the souls caught in the unseen battle that rages around us every day. We pray for the universal Church's needs, for public authorities, for those burdened by difficulties, for the end of abortion, for our local community, and so on. We do this as a response to God's invitation to pray in and with the Church.[66]

---

[65] *General Instruction of the Roman Missal*, 69.

[66] Regarding the importance of the priesthood, let us be sure to pray the prayer below for an increase in vocations:

O God, Father of all mercies,
Provider of a bountiful harvest,
send Your graces upon those
You have called to gather the fruits of Your labor;
preserve and strengthen them in their lifelong
    service of You.

Open the hearts of Your children
that they may discern Your Holy Will;

As we reflect on the dying and rising of Christ, we ought to reflect on the word "offering." Growing up, I heard the term a lot, so much so that I grew to dislike it and the whole idea of "offering." Often, I would hear the term while enduring some trial or tribulation. You can well imagine, the last thing I wanted to hear during my pain was "Offer it up," and yet this is precisely what I heard.

As I grew older, I started to do my homework and found the passages I have been sharing with you in these last two chapters —passages that speak of redemptive suffering and our call to offer our lives as sacrifices of praise. As it turns out, the more I studied this topic, the more I heard Christ *from the Cross* say to me, "Offer it up." I discovered it was not chance (nothing ever is) that the words "Offer it up" were being echoed in my ears during my excruciation—for excruciation and offering belong together. The term "excruciating" comes from the Latin *ex-cruces*, meaning "from the Cross." As Christ offers His excruciation to God the Father from the Cross, He says to each of us, "Offer it up"—not as an imposition, but as an invitation to share in the vast, mysterious power of His one mediation (see 1 Tim. 2:1–5 and Col. 1:24).[67] On the Cross, Christ redeemed suffering from

inspire in them a love and desire to surrender themselves to serving others in the name of Your Son, Jesus Christ.

Teach all Your faithful to follow their respective paths
in life, guided by Your Divine Word and Truth.
Through the intercession of the Most Blessed Virgin Mary,
all the angels, and saints, hear our humble prayers
and grant Your Church's needs, through Christ, our Lord.
Amen.

[67] We are more than the sum of our excruciating pains and losses. We are first and foremost children of God whom the Father loves with an excruciating passion. He desires that we invite Him into those pains and losses so He can heal them with His

loss and despair. For this reason, our suffering that we experience as loss and despair, when united to Christ in the Spirit, is now victorious. Christ's invitation into His mediation brings us into the "Thou" of God, into the space where all offerings find their enrichment. By meditating on Christ's offering and entering into the "Thou" of God, we discover that in "offering it up," we do not go it alone! We unlock the secret of offering in the spiritual power gained from giving our pain to God for the sake of our petitions.

How does all this take place? Let us briefly consider the distinction between objective redemption and subjective redemption. Objective redemption is the historical work of the Cross, the graces obtained by the merits of Jesus Christ for the forgiveness of sins, a once-and-for-all work. Subjective redemption is how those graces are released upon every person in every generation, including our own life and current age. In other words, when we unite our suffering with the suffering of Christ, we do not obtain graces for the soul we are praying for—that has already been accomplished—but we help release the graces already merited by Jesus Christ. This distinction between obtaining and releasing is essential because it highlights the importance of including a prayer for the heart of the person we are praying for. Here again, the heart matters, and praying for an opening of the heart to receive God's graces is essential to the work of redemptive suffering.

So, as we take our petitions of intercession and place them on the altar—intentionally offering them to God—we pray with confidence that the Holy Spirit will transform their substance into

---

excruciating love. Also, when discerned and appropriate, there are times when God calls us to encourage those for whom we are praying to enter the dynamism of redemptive suffering as well (see Col. 1:24).

something new and beautiful to behold, just as He does with the offering of the Mass.

Tip 2: Praise Unceasingly, Praise in Song

In addition to the Eucharistic reference, the author of the Letter to the Hebrews says that our praise of thanksgiving is unceasing. Our song to the Lord does not end with the Liturgy but becomes a way of life. Saint Paul writes to the Church in Ephesus, "Be filled with the Spirit, addressing one another in psalms and hymns and spiritual songs, singing and making melody to the Lord with all your heart, *always and for everything giving thanks* in the name of our Lord Jesus Christ to God the Father" (Eph. 5:18–20, emphasis added). Saint Paul wants our Eucharistic thanksgiving to spill over into our everyday life as unceasing praise! Incessant praise enriches our perpetual courtship with God.[68]

Praise is an everyday occurrence. We praise many people and things. I have praised athletes, actors and actresses, musicians, my kids, and so on. We find it necessary to laud achievement, extol the fruit of hard work, and acclaim excellence because, as C. S. Lewis reminds us, "We delight to praise what we enjoy.... The praise not merely expresses but completes the enjoyment; it is its appointed consummation."[69] We praise God not to satisfy His ego but because our enjoyment of Him would otherwise be incomplete.

---

[68] As I noted in *A Heart for Evangelizing*, if you take the total number of priests and do the math, four Masses are being celebrated every second of every day. In this sense, Liturgy itself offers perpetual praise (26–27).

[69] C. S. Lewis, *Reflections on the Psalms*, 2nd ed. (Orlando, FL: Harvest Books, 1986), 95.

Unleashing the Power of Intercessory Prayer

In an active prayer life, praise is the enjoyment of God's presence and the simultaneous lifting of the whole of the interior life, our innermost self, to Him—often manifested in song and shouting (see Isa. 12:5; Ps. 9:11; 33:1; 98:4). In fact, the verb "to sing" is one of the most common verses in all the Bible.[70]

A sure sign that the Holy Spirit dwells within us is the ease with which we thank God for His blessings, and as the psalms show us, the Holy Spirit often inspires this praise and thanksgiving through song. In this sense, inspired song is a love language of heaven. Whether you think you have a good or bad voice, God desires to hear it; He's the one who gave it to you.

Praise in song is a beautiful manifestation of the divine indwelling and a lovely way to place our prayers of intercession before God. Here, I would like to make three suggestions on how to praise God better. These are merely invitations to enter deeper into the delight of God.

First, *chant the Divine Office*. The Divine Office, otherwise known as the Breviary or the Liturgy of the Hours, involves praying Scripture, especially the psalms. Included in the Divine Office are canticles and readings from the Church Fathers and spiritual masters. Seen as an extension of the Eucharist, the Divine Office has always been an essential prayer of the Church. As part of the Church's ancient practice, the psalms were chanted, as they were meant to be prayed.

In the Morning Prayer and Evening Prayer sections of the Divine Office, there are times of prescribed intercessions—excellent times to hold up your petitions of intercession before God and, as you are inspired, do so in song. It is a beautiful way of responding to the inquiry "Will you pray for me?"[71]

---

[70] See Joseph Ratzinger, *The Spirit of the Liturgy* (San Francisco: Ignatius Press, 2000), 125.

[71] Saint Benedict called the Liturgy of the Hours the work of God (the *Opus Dei*)—the work God is doing in you when you pray.

Second, *sing the Litany of the Saints.* This is a favorite devotional of mine. There is something intensely moving about calling upon the intercession of the saints in the form of a litany. One of my favorite parts of the Rite of the Ordination of Priests occurs when the newly ordained priest lies prostrate on the church floor while the Litany of the Saints is sung. There are few times I have felt closer to heaven than when singing the Litany of Saints during the Rite of Ordination.

In my everyday life, I have made the earnest effort to include something like this in the Hollcraft home. Each of my four children has a saint he or she calls upon, and the Hollcraft family ends their nightly prayer with a litany to our chosen saints.

Calling upon the saints in song is another powerful way to intercede on behalf of your brother or sister in Christ. Here, it might be helpful to ask your friend if he or she has a devotion to a particular saint. If not, help your friend select one that fits his or her charism or need. Then include the saint in your litany and ask that saint to pray for your friend.

Hebrews 12:1 reminds us (as illustrated on the cover of this book) that "so great a cloud of witnesses" surrounds us — the saints — and they are cheering us on from the stands of heaven. As the book of Revelation records, the saints have a favored intercession in the one mediation of Christ (see Rev. 5:8; 8:3–5).

Third, *praise God with your favorite Christian and Catholic songs.* This can be done individually in your house, in your car, in the shower, or on a walk. Yes, God desires praise anywhere and everywhere, even in your shower. I recently went for a walk along a water channel and witnessed a young woman singing a song, and I assure you she was praising God in it. Praising God can also be done communally, at a house or local parish. For readers of this book who have experienced communal praise — for example, festivals of praise — you know what kind of impact this can have on your life of intercessory prayer. When you sing, mentally insert the petition in your heart, and let your song be an offering of intercessory praise. To lift your voice is then to lift your petition of intercession. In this, we become intercessors in praise.

Tip 3: Infuse Gratitude into Your Intercession

Lastly, to practice the prayer of thankfulness is to practice the virtue of gratitude. With the practice of gratitude in our everyday lives, the habit of being thankful in prayer becomes more natural.

As a nation, at least for one day, we practice this virtue quite well. On Thanksgiving Day, we come together to celebrate family life as we gather around the dinner table to pray, eat, and tell our favorite memories. Typically, on this day, we give to those who have less because we appreciate that we have more. People of faith celebrate God's revelation with greater vigor than usual. It is a holiday (a "holy-day") because it is the day on which we express our gratitude for who we are; what we have in faith, family, and friends; and what we can do for others.

But what if Thanksgiving Day were more than just one day? What if it were a way of life? What if it were *the* way of intercessory prayer? Christ desires that we be grateful in season and out of season—especially when "out of season" is three hundred sixty-four days of the year.

When Jesus healed ten lepers, and only one returned giving thanks to God, Christ asked, "Were there not ten cleansed?" (see Luke 17:11–19). "Strange," I'm sure He thought, "I just transformed the lives of ten lepers and only one returned to say 'thank you.'" At the very least, when God has done something extraordinary for us, we should say "thank you." We ought to give thanks and count our blessings—taking stock of who we are; what we have in faith, family, and friends; and what we can do for others. This "taking stock," and the life that springs from it, is the way of gratitude—a form of paying closer attention to God.

Let us bring this habitual expression of gratitude into our petitions of intercession. Offering up prayers of gratitude enables God to release a kind of loveliness and graciousness over our supplication. For example, when we pray for a friend's daughter who has been diagnosed with cancer, we offer up prayers of thanksgiving for the gift of our faith, the gift of the Cross, the gift of our friend and her daughter, and for what God is doing in their lives. At this point, we pray with fervor that God works in the soul for whom we are praying.

As a father, my heart is *always* deeply moved when my children say "thank you." If I am so moved, we can be assured that the heart of God, our Father, is moved exponentially more. God the Father smiles over all situations that express thanksgiving, and as He smiles, He releases more grace over the whole of our prayer—"grace upon grace" from the fullness of God (see John 1:16). What you feed grows; therefore, gratitude begets more gratitude.

However, saying "thank you" and expressing gratitude can be one of the more difficult things to do. Maybe we are holding a grudge. If so, we should not foster it; we should choose to forgive. The virtue of gratitude is set free when we stop holding grudges. The less we are bound to our resentments, the more available our hearts are to serve God and praise Him in gratitude.

Live Thanksgiving every day and infuse gratitude into your petitions of intercession.

Key Patron: Saint Kateri Tekakwitha

Among the many saints who infused gratitude into their devoted intercessory prayer was "the princess of the Eucharist"—Saint Kateri Tekakwitha.

Unleashing the Power of Intercessory Prayer

The first Native American to be declared a saint, Delia Tekak-witha was born in 1656 to an Algonquin woman who married the Mohawk clan's chief in what is today upstate New York. At the tender age of four, she lost her entire family to a smallpox breakout and was adopted by her uncle, the new chief of the Mohawk clan.

Delia's early years were marked by the struggle to find her identity after being struck with smallpox and orphaned. The smallpox breakout had left her with permanent facial scars that drove her to cover her face with a blanket. Also, Kateri had to navigate her adopted parents' desire to arrange her marriage. At the age of twenty, she would discover the identity for which she was destined.

In 1676, Delia's life took a dramatic turn when a Jesuit missionary baptized her into the Catholic Faith. She took the name Kateri (Mohawk for "Catherine") after Saint Catherine of Siena. After her Baptism, she embraced wholeheartedly her new identity in the image of the Creator and clothed with the garment of virtue (see Col. 3:10, 12).

Her new identity brought her interior peace, but becoming Catholic opened her to even more exterior ridicule and persecution from the village. In one case, for not working on a Sunday, the village refused to feed her. Eventually, under the spiritual direction of the local missionary priest, she was encouraged to flee to Canada. She followed his guidance and journeyed two hundred miles to a mission in Montreal near the Saint Lawrence River. There she made a vow of virginity and devoted the final four years of life to prayer, service to the poor, and teaching her clan the way of Christ. She brought many Mohawk Indians into the Catholic Faith.

Kateri's time just outside Montreal was marked notably by her deep devotion to Jesus in the Blessed Sacrament. While she had chiefs for her biological and adopted fathers, it was to the Chieftain Jesus Christ that she pledged her greatest love and loyalty. She received our Lord in the Eucharist every day.

Ultimately, Kateri's love for Jesus Christ in the Eucharist deepened her intercessory prayer and led her to offer many fasts for the conversion of her people. The more she prayed, the more she received the fruits of the Eucharist. She began to see that praying for the souls who persecuted her was a sharing in the mystery of the Cross. Hers was a life of prayer that existed for others.

Kateri died on April 17, 1680, at the age of twenty-four. A French priest by the name of Father Pierre Cholenec witnessed something extraordinary at her deathbed. He states:

> Her face ... so disfigured and so swarthy in life, suddenly changed about fifteen minutes after her death, and in an instant became so beautiful and so fair that just as soon as I saw it I let out a yell, I was so astonished, and I sent for the priest who was working at the repository for the Holy Thursday service. At the news of this prodigy, he came running along with some people who were with him. We then had the time to contemplate this marvel right up to the time of her burial. I frankly admit that my first thought at the time was that Catherine could well have entered heaven at that moment and that she had—as a preview—already received in her virginal body a small indication of the glory of which her soul had taken possession in Heaven.[72]

The news of the scars disappearing from Kateri's face spread like wildfire. The radiance of Christ's light emanating from Kateri inspired numerous conversions from the darkness of sin. Indeed, Kateri was taken to heaven, where she would become a powerful intercessor for the people of God. Known as the "lily of the Mohawk

---

[72] Kathy Schiffer, "St. Kateri Tekakwitha, the Lily of the Mohawks," National Catholic Register, July 14, 2020, http://www.ncregister. com/blog/kschiffer/st.-kateri-tekakwitha-the-lily-of-the-mohawks.

people," Kateri Tekakwitha was beatified in 1980 by Pope John Paul II and canonized in 2012 by Pope Benedict XVI.

Saint Kateri is the patron saint for people who are ridiculed for their piety. Let us call upon her intercession if we ever find ourselves exiled for pursuing holiness and praying for others in a world that downplays the power of intercessory prayer.

As a Native American, Kateri's name often comes up at Thanksgiving; this is very fitting because of her deep devotion to the Eucharist, which in the Greek (*eucharistesas*) means "thanksgiving." When we go on bended knee in Mass to pray for the souls who have entrusted their requests to us, we would be well served to recommend those petitions to the prayers of Saint Kateri Tekakwitha.

Saint Kateri, pray for us!

Prompt Questions for Journaling

1. Do you enter into the mystery of the Mass as the great prayer of eternal intercession that it is? Do you remember to offer to God all your petitions of intercession? Reflect.
2. What are your favorite Catholic songs? Do you pray these songs as a form of intercessory prayer? Reflect.

9

Pray with Mary

Over the last five hundred years, scientists and doctors have visited such cities as Pontmain, France; Beauraing, Belgium; Banneux, Belgium; and Zion, Italy. These scientists, some claiming to be agnostic, some atheist, discovered an unexpected smell, a fragrance, a sweet perfume, unlike anything they had ever encountered. Other scientists found these scents in places such as Knock, Ireland; Fatima, Portugal; Lourdes, France; Kibeho, Rwanda; Zaitun, Egypt; and Tenochtitlan (Mexico City), Mexico. What did these experts in the field of physical science find? An aroma that came not from the earth but from heaven—from Mary, the Mother of God.

Among these professionals was the popular French doctor Luc Montagnier, a Nobel Prize winner in medicine (2008) and the physician credited with discovering HIV. When asked in an interview about the Marian apparition at Lourdes, he answered, "When a phenomenon is inexplicable, if it really exists, then there's no reason to deny it.... In the miracles of Lourdes, there is something inexplicable."[73] As of February 11, 2018 (feast of Our Lady

---

[73] "Nobel Prize–Winning Agnostic Scientist Says: "The Miracles at Lourdes Are Inexplicable," Aleteia, February 18, 2017, https://

of Lourdes), there have been seventy healings that physical science cannot explain, but only the healing power of God.

Off and on for five centuries, Mary has been appearing, bringing with her not only a divine fragrance, but also a heavenly message: Believe, repent, pray, fast, and give alms! For five centuries, the Blessed Virgin Mary has been resounding the gospel message to us, her children. For five centuries, Mary has been flying to our aid.

Mary flies to our aid because this is what mothers do when their children are in trouble.

Intercessory Key: Pray with Mary

This last key is one that lies at the heart of the Gospel. God chose Mary as a mediator, and so should we. We read Mary as mediator throughout the Gospel narratives. Matthew introduces us to Mary as the Virgin who will "conceive and bear a son" (Matt. 1:23)—the Son who is the God-Man, Jesus Christ (see 1 Tim. 2:5). Luke introduces us to Mary in the Annunciation with the great angelic salutation: "Hail, full of grace ... " (Luke 1:28). After a brief dialogue about "How shall this be" (Luke 1:34), Mary says "yes" to the vocation of being the Mother of God. John introduces us to Mary at the Wedding Feast at Cana with her words "They have no wine" (John 2:3). After a dialogue between Mary and her Son, Mary tells the servants, "Do whatever he tells you" (John 2:5), and Jesus turns water into wine. The first miracle performed by Jesus in the Gospel is due to the direct mediation of Mary. If we desire to do the same—make Jesus uniquely present and prompt His action—through our intercessory prayer, we ought to place our petitions into the immaculate hands of Mary (see Luke 1:28)

aleteia.org/2017/02/18/nobel-prize-winning-agnostic-scientist-says -the-miracles-at-lourdes-are-inexplicable.

and allow her to turn them over to her Son. We ask people whom we perceive are close to Jesus to pray for us. Could we find anyone closer to Jesus than Mary?

When we pray with Mary, we pray with Christ, for their intentions are one and the same.

Tip 1: Pray the Memorare

I used to dream of flying, of soaring through the air, capable of going from one place to another in a matter of seconds. I wanted to fly so badly that one day I decided to spread my arms wide and jump from a two-story roof. Sadly, I didn't take off flying and was instead rushed to the hospital with a broken arm.

Among other things, psychologists suggest that a boy's desire to fly has something to do with exercising his freedom and being a "hero." Praying for others is a beautiful exercise of our *freedom* and an act of *heroism* as it puts others before the self—and heroes are admired for their willingness to place the safety and well-being of others before their own. Jesus invites us to *freely choose* Mary (see John 19:25–27) in the act of counting ourselves second in intercessory prayer. Certainly, intercessory prayer is a heroic act. So let us fly to Mary in our intercessory prayer.

There are prayers of intercession, and then there is the Memorare—the great plea to Mary. In this great plea, we pray:

> Remember O most gracious Virgin Mary that never was it known that anyone who fled to your protection, implored your help, or sought your intercession, was left unaided.
>
> Inspired with this confidence, I fly to you, O Virgin of virgins, my Mother; to you do I come, before you I stand, sinful and sorrowful.
>
> O Mother of the Word Incarnate, despise not my petitions, but in your mercy hear and answer me. Amen.

In the first stanza of this twelfth-century prayer,[74] we petition Mary, our advocate in the courtroom of grace, never to abandon us in our time of need. If human mothers do not forget their children, how much more will our Divine Mother "remember us in our time of need." We pray, "O most gracious Virgin Mary," because she is perfectly courteous and benevolent. Mary is the highly favored one, the one "full of grace" (Luke 1:28).

Many saints, including Francis de Sales and Mother Teresa of Calcutta, prayed the Memorare every day. In the case of Mother Teresa, she "flew" to the bosom of the Blessed Virgin Mary by way of the Memorare nine consecutive times each day.

The second stanza of the Memorare — "Inspired with this confidence, I fly to you, O Virgin of virgins, my Mother; to you do I come, before you I stand, sinful and sorrowful" — is a prayer of faith ("with this confidence") and humility ("to you do I come, before you I stand, sinful and sorrowful"). Are we flying to the Blessed Virgin with faith and humility?

One of the hidden gems of praying for others is that it calls us to become more Christlike. The words "to you do I come, before you I stand" verbalize the action that the heart takes to "move toward" and "arrive at" the feet of Mary in prayer. We live in a world of "I almost" and "I started to." We say things like "I almost helped the homeless person on the street; or "I started to get up and go to Confession, but ..." In this classic Marian prayer, we do more than "almost" or "start to." In faith, we get up and go to Mary, stand before her, and humbly place ourselves and our petitions in her care.

Sinful and *sorrowful*, we go before Mary. We are all sinners in need of God's mercy. "If we say we have no sin, we deceive ourselves, and the truth is not in us" (1 John 1:8). Sin is disobedience to God, and

[74] The Memorare comes from the larger prayer "At Your Holy Feet, Most Sweet Virgin Mary."

worse yet, sin breaks God the Father's heart. By showing remorse for our sin (spiritual sorrow), and receiving His merciful grace in the sacrament of Confession, we are restored to our proper relationship with God, divine intimacy with Him.

The more we appropriate the words we pray, the more humbly we pray: "O Mother of the Word Incarnate, despise not my petitions, but in your mercy hear and answer me." This final stanza contains a great crying out. A mother is always attentive to the cry of her child, and we can be assured that when we cry to our heavenly Mother, she "despises not" our petitions but listens attentively. Mary is a captive audience to our prayer, and her deepest desire is to fly to our aid!

In this ending stanza, a question often arises: "Is it proper to pray to Mary with the words 'in your mercy?'" After all, it is the merciful heart of Christ that saved man from sin. The short answer is: yes, it is proper. It is proper because Mary shares in the one mediation of Christ in a unique way, and this uniqueness shines forth in the office of mercy. What do I mean? Here we need to turn our attentions to Sacred Scripture.

During Israel's monarchy, the mother of the king would share in her son's reign, serving as an advocate for the people and as a counselor for her son. We see this concretely with Bathsheba, wife of King David and the mother to his successor, King Solomon. We read in 1 Kings 2:16–20:

[Adonijah said to Bathsheba,] "And now I have one request to make of you; do not refuse me." She said to him, "Say on." And he said, "Pray ask King Solomon—he will not refuse you—to give me Abishag the Shunammite as my wife." Bathsheba said, "Very well; I will speak for you to the king." So Bathsheba went to King Solomon, to speak to him on behalf of Adonijah. And the king rose to meet her, and bowed down to her; then he sat on his throne, and had a seat brought for the king's mother; and she sat on his right. Then she said, "I have one small request to make of you; do not refuse me." And the king said to her, "Make your request, my mother; for I will not refuse you."

Another rendering of the text, "Do not refuse me" is "Do not turn away my face." King Solomon honored his mother by rising to meet her and bowing down to her. He did not turn away his face, but listened carefully to her petition.

This passage shows an encounter between a mother, Bathsheba, and her son-king, Solomon, and prefigures the encounters between another mother, Mary, and her Son-King, Jesus. Imagine taking your petition to Mary with the same confidence as Adonijah took to Bathsheba. Do we stand before Mary in the same way, certain that her Son will listen attentively to our petition when Mary speaks on our behalf? Mary will say to us, as Bathsheba said to Adonijah, "Very well, I will speak for you to the King," and her Son-King will say to her, as Solomon said to Bathsheba, "Make your request, my Mother, for I will not refuse to listen to you." We should imitate this confidence as we bring our intercessions before Mary.

As stated previously, sometimes we ask specific individuals for their prayers because we can sense how close they are to Jesus. Of all the saints, Mary is the closest to Jesus, and so it makes sense that we would make a special effort to ask for her intercession. Mary takes our petition and places it before her Son-King, and He grants her request *according to His divine plan.* Mary is the new advocate in the new Kingdom of David; she is the Queen Mother of the Almighty King.

In light of Mary as Queen Mother, we should let the words of Mary's cousin Elizabeth echo in our ears: "And why is this granted me, that the mother of my Lord should come to me?" (Luke 1:43). The Hebrew word for "mother of my Lord," *Gebireh,* is used in the Old Testament to describe Bathsheba, the "queen-mother."

This word also means "great lady." Mary is the Great Lady who intercedes on our behalf as the Queen-Mother. May we have great confidence in her intercession!

Pray the Memorare as often as possible, or at least as often as someone asks you for prayers. (This is a great prayer to pray "on the spot" with the one who has requested your prayers.)

As we fly to Mary in prayer, she will teach us how to pray better, which includes a call to "ponder" as she did (Luke 2:19; see 2:51). Understanding Mary's pondering is an excellent next step for us as we seek to deepen our intercessory prayer.

Tip 2: Ponder

We think carefully about many things. We deliberate over everything from political policies to favorite movies. Deliberation takes many forms within many matters every day, but what of God and Mary? Do we think carefully about God? How do we ponder? Do we ponder as Mary did?

The Gospel of Luke reveals a compelling connection between Mary's pondering and our intercessory prayer.[75] There we read, "And [the shepherds] went with haste, and found Mary and Joseph, and the babe lying in a manger. And when they saw it they made known the saying which had been told them concerning this child; and all who heard it wondered at what the shepherds told them. But Mary kept all these things, pondering them in her heart" (2:16–19). After this narrative, some thirty verses later, Luke records the episode in which Mary finds Jesus after He has been lost for three days. When Mary and Joseph found Jesus in the Temple, Jesus "said to them, 'How is it that you sought me? Did you not know that I must be in my Father's house?' And they did

[75] See Hollcraft, *A Heart for Evangelizing*, 144.

not understand the saying which he spoke to them. And he went down with them and came to Nazareth, and was obedient to them; and his mother kept all these things in her heart" (2:49–51). In each narrative, we read of Mary's thinking carefully, pondering the mysterious events unfolding before her.

The Greek word for "pondering," *symballein*, means "to throw together, to compare and weigh facts," or "to piece together." Indeed, Mary had to "think carefully," weighing her vow of virginity against her calling to bear the Son of God. She had to "piece together" the wider meaning of losing God for three days with finding Him in the Temple. What we see in Mary's pondering is a weighing and a piecing together of the divine workings of God. If we seek to understand His plan, then we ought to learn to ponder as Mary did.

In practicing pondering in our intercessory prayer, we take up the practice of defeating the Enemy! There is a fascinating word juxtaposition that appears in the Greek. The Greek *symballein* (to throw together) is in direct contrast with the Greek *diaballein*, which means "to throw across; to scatter." From *diaballein* we get the English word *diabolical*, which we often translate as "belonging to Satan." Satan's function is to leave us "scattered"—thrown asunder, confused about everyday life. We overcome the tempter's tactics by "piecing together"—making sense of, in God's grace, what God desires us to make sense of. In many cases, as in intercessory prayer, God inspires us to help others make sense of difficult situations by sharing prayerful insights with those who have asked us to pray for them. We overcome Satan's *diaballein* by imitating Mary's *symballein* and by helping others to do so as well. Indeed, there is enmity between Mary and Satan (see Gen. 3:15); hers is the way to combat the enemy most effectively.

One of the most powerful tools of Marian prayer we can use is the Holy Rosary. With it, we practice pondering by meditating on the mysteries of the Rosary: the Joyful, the Sorrowful, the Glorious, and the Luminous.[76] Each set of mysteries allows us to pray by focusing our minds on specific events in the lives of Jesus and Mary. As we ponder these events in Sacred Scripture, we encounter God speaking to us and potentially speaking to the person or situation we are praying for. For example, if we are praying for the conversion of a loved one, and we are meditating upon the Third Luminous Mystery, the Proclamation of the Kingdom of God, God might encourage us to share an insight from the Beatitudes (see Matt. 5:1–12) in the Sermon on the Mount (see Matt. 5–7). By passing on insight gained from your meditation, you can aid in the work of conversion! Pondering with Mary has the power to yield great spiritual gifts for ourselves and for others.

What's more, as we pray each Hail Mary, we echo Mary's *fiat* —her great "yes" to be the Mother of God!

Tip 3: Say "Yes"

The course of Mary's pondering was made possible because she first said "yes" to the will of God. "Today's yes," says C.S. Lewis, "is the capture of a strategic point from which, a few months later, you may be able to go on to victories you never dreamed of."[77] By victories, C.S. Lewis means advancing toward the prize of heaven. Today's "yes" to the will of God makes possible the next "yes" to the will of God, which is to say, we will never know the wonderful adventure of tomorrow's "yes" without our "yes" of today.

In Tolkien's famous book *The Lord of the Rings*, Samwise would have never experienced Middle Earth's heaven in Rivendell, the

---

[76] The Joyful Mysteries are usually prayed on Mondays and Saturdays, the Sorrowful Mysteries on Tuesdays and Fridays, the Glorious Mysteries on Wednesdays and Sundays, and the Luminous Mysteries on Thursdays.

[77] C.S. Lewis, *Mere Christianity* (New York: Macmillan, 1952), 117.

trek to Mount Doom with Frodo, or sailing to the Undying Lands[78] if he did not first say "yes" to the path put before him in the Shire. For Samwise, sailing off to the Undying Lands was made possible because he first said "yes" to leaving the Shire and helping Frodo destroy the One Ring. Frodo, Samwise, and the whole Fellowship of the Ring went on to a great victory that had been unimaginable at the point when they gave their initial "yes."

For Mary, her Assumption to the "Undying Lands" (heaven) was made possible because she first said "yes" to God's plan; she said "yes" to bringing the Child Jesus into the world. Jesus, Mary, and the whole fellowship of the Apostles went on to great victories because they said "yes" to the first step of the great adventure of conquering the power of death in the world. The first "yes" step can be quite modest but eventually leads to great outcomes—as the fruit of obedience often does.

Samwise's quiet "yes" in the Shire led him to a mountaintop (Mount Doom) where he would experience earthquakes, peals of thunder, and the eventual transformation of Middle Earth. Mary's quiet "yes" in Nazareth led her to a mountaintop (Calvary) where she would experience earthquakes, peals of thunder, and the eventual transformation of the world. Samwise's "yes" led to the redemption of a fictional world; Mary's "yes" led to the redemption of the very world in which we live.

What do the exploits of Samwise and Mary teach us about intercession? A lot! Samwise steadily stood by Frodo's side to save Middle Earth. Mary tirelessly gave of herself to be at the service of the mission of her Son. From their initial "yeses," their lives served as mediations, petitions of intercession in the form of offering their lives for something greater than themselves.

---

[78] See "Later Events concerning the Members of the Fellowship of the Ring," 1482, in appendix 2 in *The Lord of the Rings*.

We, like Samwise and Mary, are called to devoted, intercessory companionship. If you are married, you have already given an initial "yes" to a great adventure in which you are a mediator and an intercessor who lays down your life for the other. When others ask us to pray for them, we initially respond by internalizing their requests and praying for them on a regular basis, as we have explored. However, at times, God may want greater commitment, even giving the whole of our lives to someone, as Samwise did and as Mary did—even if it involves climbing up rocky-edged mountains.

We live in the nonfictional version of redemption, and we have roles in the redemption of our nonfictional world. We must play our parts in this redemption by saying "yes" to God every moment that we can. By doing so, we bring His light and His salvation to the darkness of evil in the world. We enable this light to come into the world by first letting it inhabit ourselves, as Mary did.

Reflecting on the stories of Samwise and Mary, we ought to ask a couple of questions: How will our stories be remembered? Will they include a willing surrender modeled by Samwise and the Blessed Virgin Mary? On a regular basis, we ought to draw back from our regular routines to "take stock" of how we will be remembered.

How we are remembered was an important question for Sam. As Sam and Frodo were moving closer to Mount Doom, they were musing over how they would be recalled:

SAM. I wonder if we'll ever be put into songs or tales.

FRODO [turns around]. What?

SAM. I wonder if people will ever say, "Let's hear about Frodo and the Ring." And they'll say, "Yes, that's one of my favorite stories. Frodo was really brave, wasn't he, Dad?"

"Yes, my boy, the most famousest of hobbits. And that's saying a lot."

FRODO [continuing walking]. You've left out one of the chief characters—Samwise the stouthearted. I want to hear more about Sam. Why didn't they put in more of his talk, Dad? Frodo wouldn't have gotten far without Sam, would he, Dad?"

SAM. Now, Mr. Frodo, you shouldn't make fun; I was being serious.

FRODO. So was I.[79]

According to Frodo, Samwise will be remembered for his stout-hearted bravery and his willingness to stick his neck out on behalf of others. Mary stuck her neck out for the sake of others, and it led her to becoming the Mother of God. We tend to remember the saints for their Tolkien acts of heroism as well. Saint Francis of Assisi can just as well be Saint Francis the Stouthearted, and Saint Mother Teresa of Calcutta be Saint Mother Teresa the Stout-hearted. Where will sticking our neck out for others lead us? By the grace of God, will I be remembered as "Joseph the Stouthearted?" Or you, as "[insert your name here] the Stouthearted?"

In my heart, I believe that every person who met Saint Francis of Assisi could say, like Frodo, "I wouldn't have gotten very far without Saint Francis." In my heart, I believe any person who met any of the (roughly) eleven thousand saints "wouldn't have gotten very far" without them. In fact, saints became saints be-cause of other saints. For example, Saint Ignatius of Loyola was inspired to bravery by the story of Saint Benedict of Nursia and his willingness to surrender his life to Jesus Christ. Beyond our "yes"

[79] J.R.R. Tolkien, *The Lord of the Rings*, pt. 2, *The Two Towers* (New York: Ballantine Books, 1965), 363–364.

to God is a meeting—a meeting between you and another. Will the other say, "I would not have gotten very far without [insert your name here]?"

Say "yes" to God "with all your heart and with all your soul and with all your strength and with all your mind" (Luke 10:27). As you do this, loving your neighbor as yourself (see Luke 10:27) will become a way to best intercede for your fellow man with your whole life. Mary taught us as much, so let us follow her lead.

Lastly, in what stands as Mary's iconic "yes"—"let it be done to me" (Luke 1:38)—we have some important words both to contemplate and follow. After the initial angelic salutation (see Luke 1:28), and before she said "yes," the angel Gabriel assured Mary that nothing is impossible in the power of God (see Luke 1:37). Like Mary, we are to transform our imaginings into reality by saying "yes" to the Holy Spirit and becoming mediators of the impossible. After having received the Holy Spirit ("overshadowed"), she "arose and went" (Luke 1:39) to be at the service of intercession—mediating the good news of Jesus Christ. Similarly, after we have invited the Holy Spirit into our lives, the Paraclete will inspire us to intercede on behalf of the good news of Jesus Christ.

Moreover, the Greek rendering of this phrase "Let it be to me according to your word" is *genoito*, which implies that Mary was joyfully receptive to the angel's invitation. The word can translate as a joyful desire to do God's will. Mary does not begrudgingly submit to God's plan but enthusiastically embraces it. Inside Mary's response is a total surrender and abandonment to God, but one that is moved entirely by a desire to love, bringing God's eternal design to fruition here on earth.

Let us be imitators of Mary, the one whose "yes" gives penultimate meaning to all intercession. Indeed, her "yes" made possible the greatest victory in human history: the triumph of the Cross!

Unleashing the Power of Intercessory Prayer

Key Patron: Saint Louis de Montfort

I say the name Saint Augustine, and what do we think of? Probably something related to his conversion story of playboy to priest. I say the name Saint Francis of Assisi, and what thought holds our attention? Undoubtedly, his relationship with animals. I say the name Saint Mother Teresa of Calcutta, and we immediately have the poorest of the poor on our minds. There are some saints in the history of the Catholic Church who are synonymous with something or someone tied to the saints' charisms. We read about Saint Augustine and are hopeful that we will be able to overcome our worst sin and do great things for God. We read about Saint Francis of Assisi, and our appreciation for creation is renewed. We read about Saint Mother Teresa of Calcutta and realize that caring for the poor, for our children, for those in need lies at the heart of our Catholic Faith.

Following this reflection, I say the name Saint Louis de Montfort, and immediately Mary comes to mind. The more familiar we become with Saint Louis de Montfort, the more familiar we become with Mary. His commitment to her was so strong that he took up the motto *Totus tuus ego sum* ("I am all yours") to express his devotion to Mary.[80]

Born in France in the late seventeenth century, Saint Louis de Montfort lived his love for the poor. Alongside his commitment to service (corporal works of mercy), and after his ordination at

---

[80] Saint John Paul II also had a devotion to Mary. Influenced by the life and writings of Saint Louis de Montfort, the great pope had *totus tuus* (entirely yours) "stamped" on his papal crest. Saint John Paul II consecrated the entirety of his papacy to the Blessed Virgin Mary. Another Polish saint from the twentieth century who consecrated his life to Mary was Saint Maximilian Kolbe. As treated in the opening chapter, he became a great intercessor for the people of God—quite literally "standing in between" (intercession) an SS agent and a prisoner.

the age of twenty-seven, he fell in love with the call to preach and instruct the ignorant (spiritual work of mercy).

The preaching of Father Louis de Montfort emanated great devotion to and love for Mary. As time passed, his popularity grew, but so did oppositions to his preaching.

Early eighteenth-century France was heavily influenced by the heresy of Jansenism. Among other things, Jansenism claimed the teaching of predestination: that God actively bestows grace on some while actively withholding it from others. It claimed that only a few are saved, and that everyone else is damned. Father Louis de Montfort was preaching the message that true devotion to Mary is instrumental for the salvation of *all* souls. So enraged were the French Jansenists that they poisoned Father Louis de Montfort. It was then, while recovering from being poisoned, that he penned his classic work, *True Devotion to Mary* — arguably the most significant work ever written on Marian spirituality.

At the heart of de Montfort's book lies the key to developing a Marian spirituality: consecration to Jesus through Mary. What does this consecration look like? And why is it of great value in our intercessory prayer? First, let us consider what we mean when we use the word "consecration."

The term "consecration" comes from the Latin *consecrare*, which translates as "to make holy, devote." This comes from the assimilated form of *cum*, meaning "with, together," and *sacrare*, "to make or declare sacred." In principle, consecration is the action taken to become more holy in devoted service to God. This begins at Baptism. By virtue of our Baptism, we are consecrated to God — set apart for holiness. In the Old Testament, things such as liturgical vessels were set apart, or "consecrated," for a sacred purpose. In the New Testament, by the power of the Holy Spirit, man has been "sanctified" for holy ends (see 1 Cor. 6:11). In Baptism, we receive the holiness of God that speaks for others, a holiness that exists for their healing.

Unleashing the Power of Intercessory Prayer

Saint Louis de Montfort sets up his consecration as a plan of renewing our baptismal vows to Jesus through Mary. In a wise arrangement of stages that envisions a gradual progression of allowing God into your heart, they are as follows:[81]

- Part 1: Spirit of the World (twelve days)
- Part 2: Knowledge of Self (seven days)
- Part 3: Knowledge of Mary (seven days)
- Part 4: Knowledge of Jesus (seven days)

Note, Saint Louis de Montfort's four-step consecration taps into the ancient truth — you cannot give what you do not have — the truth that self-evangelization comes before evangelization of others. So often in life we live without identifying and overcoming the spirit of the world (see 1 Cor. 2:11–14). The spirit of the world is a denial of God's sovereignty and care — a direct denial of God that manifests itself in sin and disobedience.[82] De Montfort teaches that we must first recognize the spirit of the world and the things to which we have become attached in life before we can be at the service of another in something like intercessory prayer.

In the first nineteen days of the consecration process, the person moves toward a renewal in rejecting Satan and all his empty promises. Only then does the consecration move into a deeper understanding of the role of Mary as Mother of God and Christ as the Savior of the world. The consecration concludes with a radical "yes" to Jesus through the hands of Mary — the "yes" that affirms the call to live in God and exist for others, which includes the call to speak on behalf of others, especially when someone has asked you to do so.

Saint Louis de Montfort's charism was his love for Mary. His every waking breath was lived in Jesus through Mary. The whole

---

[81] Saint Louis de Montfort, *Total Preparation for Consecration*, 16th ed. (New York: Montfort Publication, 2001), 1.

[82] Ibid, 5.

of his life is a loud reminder that Mary was given to all of us from the Cross, and that we, too, ought to follow her closely (see John 19:25–27). So it is that we invite her into our hearts and, as we do, into our petitions of intercession.

Saint Louis de Montfort, pray for us!

Prompt Questions for Journaling

1. What role do mothers play in families? What insights can be gained by seeing Mary as Mother to the family of God, the Church?

2. What does Mary's "yes" teach us about our vocations to become intercessors of prayer?

A Suggested Prayer of Intercession

The prayer of intercession below, composed by Saint Margaret Mary Alacoque, was prayed every day by Saint Padre Pio. Among the many treasured prayers in our Deposit of Faith, I highly recommend praying this one and doing so with all the keys and tips discussed in this book.

O my Jesus, You have said: "Truly I say to you, ask and you will receive, seek and you will find, knock and it will be opened to you." Behold I knock, I seek and ask for the grace of ... (here name your request).

Our Father ... Hail Mary ... Glory Be ... Sacred Heart of Jesus, I place all my trust in You.

O my Jesus, You have said: "Truly I say to you, if you ask anything of the Father in my name, He will give it to you." Behold, in Your name, I ask the Father for the grace of ... (here name your request).

Our Father ... Hail Mary ... Glory Be ... Sacred Heart of Jesus, I place all my trust in You.

O my Jesus, You have said: "Truly I say to you, heaven and earth will pass away but my words will not pass away."

Unleashing the Power of Intercessory Prayer

Encouraged by Your infallible words, I now ask for the grace of ... (here name your request).

Our Father ... Hail Mary ... Glory Be ... Sacred Heart of Jesus, I place all my trust in You.

O Sacred Heart of Jesus, for whom it is impossible not to have compassion on the afflicted, have pity on us miserable sinners and grant us the grace which we ask of You, through the Sorrowful and Immaculate Heart of Mary, Your tender Mother and ours.

Hail, Holy Queen ... St. Joseph, foster father of Jesus, pray for us!

Conclusion

In this book, I have laid out a series of nine keys and twenty-six tips to help you better respond to the question: "Will you pray for me?" With the foundation of understanding prayer as conversation with God, we saw the value of:

- Praying in the Spirit
- Praying in faith
- Praying from the heart
- Praying fervently
- Praying on the spot
- Praying with specifics
- Praying in friendship with Christ
- Praying in thanksgiving and praise to God
- Praying with Mary

Indeed, these nine keys are imperative to fulfilling the promise we make when we say, "Yes, I will pray for you!"

Recalling my "hopes" from the preface, I pose to you some questions: Do you better understand praying for others as a vital expression of the Christian faith? Have you internalized intercessory prayer as a desire and a privilege? And most importantly, if you have begun the practice of these nine keys, has your relationship with God been strengthened?

Unleashing the Power of Intercessory Prayer

As you respond to these questions, maybe you recognize a weakness in your intercessory prayer. In this case, identify the fault and be intentional about working on it. For example, if you find yourself hesitating to pray on the spot, ask yourself, "What is holding me back?" After identifying the obstacle, begin the process of seeking to be more consistent in that area.

The value of this book lies in the practice of the nine keys. The more you pray for others, the more your heart will be opened to new insights in your prayer. While this book is not the "summa" in praying for others, I believe it is an important starting point in strengthening your intercessions (or reference point for those who have been devoted to intercessory prayer). Perhaps the Spirit will place people and situations on your heart that were not there at the beginning of your prayer. Pray for them! Perhaps, you have recognized souls who do not have to verbalize requests for prayer; you are now aware that, when your heart is adequately disposed, you can "hear" a cry for prayer in their inflection, tone, body language, and so on. Pray for those persons. Perhaps, you find yourself distracted when praying for others. Often, the very things that distract you are the very things you need to pray for! Allow your distractions to become an entry point to reengaging with your intercessory prayer. God meets us exactly where we are and walks with us exactly as He is. Pray about whatever is distracting you, and it will lead to greater intercessory prayer!

What's more, souls who prayerfully intercede for others begin to look for ways to be evangelical using their intercessory prayer. The more you practice the art of praying for others — whether it is starting a prayer chain in your local parish via social media or asking the simple question "What can I pray for?" — the more you enable yourself to build up the Kingdom of God.

My dear readers, over the years I have come to discover that we are a people who love to be surprised by lovely things. When

I receive an unexpected gift from a family member or a friend, it brings me great joy. When I surprise my wife with flowers on an ordinary day, it brings her great joy. Well, I have learned that our loving God likes to bring us great joy as well. When we invite the Holy Spirit into our lives each morning, He releases a loveliness into our day in the form of divine appointments. How many of us have prayed for someone intently that we did not know twenty-four hours ago? Maybe you met that someone you prayed for at a park, a wedding, or a ball game. How lovely is it that each day we can do a great work by praying (according to our keys) for a soul we did not know the day before! That's worth waking up for and invoking the presence of the Holy Spirit!

During the early stages of writing this book, I attended the funeral of my Uncle Frank. Growing up, I knew Uncle Frank only as a rocket scientist (literally) and a devoted fan of the professional sports teams in Oakland. I learned much more about him on the day of his funeral. As my cousin Dave offered an emotional tribute and eulogy to his father, he spoke of a man who struggled with alcoholism but overcame his addiction by virtue of Alcoholics Anonymous (AA) and God's grace. In the latter years of Uncle Frank's life, he became a sponsor with AA and realized his calling of standing in the gap between God and man as an intercessor. As the notes in the margin of his Bible suggest, he saw his vocation late in life to help other men free themselves from addiction to alcohol and, at the same time, bring people to God.

As I heard my cousin Dave reflect upon Uncle Frank's life, the question came to mind: "Was my father praying for the conversion of his brother-in-law?" I then remembered a conversation my father had with Uncle Frank that was shared with me. One night, my Uncle Frank asked my dad why he reads so many books on Catholicism. My dad responded promptly, "Within these books lie treasures for growth." My uncle Frank replied, "I think you are wasting your time." As my father shared this exchange with me, I recall asking him, "What did you say to him then, Dad?" He responded, "Nothing." I was confused. Then he said, "Joe, your Uncle Frank has a generous heart and is a good man. When we pray the Rosary each night, I entrust him to Jesus. When God sees fit, we'll have the conversations we need to have." In effect, my memory answered my question—yes, my father was praying for his brother-in-law, and he was doing so with great devotion! As it turns out, my Uncle Frank did experience a conversion to faith and became a vessel for God.

Now, was it exclusively the Rosaries my dad prayed for Uncle Frank that brought about his conversion to faith? No one will ever know, but I do believe it played a significant role in the larger narrative of his transformation. I also believe the prayers of many others led him toward conversion as well.

One soul's devotion to intercessory prayer can have a major unforeseen impact. In the infinite wisdom of God, as the storyline has played itself out in the Hollcraft family, the prayer of Father Ron for my father reached the shores and turbulent waves of my Uncle Frank's life. Would my father have devoted Rosaries for his brother-in-law if it were not for the prayer of Father Ron? This is the power of our intercessory prayer—it changes not only the lives of those we pray for but also the course of the lives of so many others!

So, with our prayers of intercession, let us change lives—one petition at a time.

About the Author

Joseph Hollcraft, Ph.D., is a professor at the Avila Institute and the director of the High Calling program there. He is the author of *A Heart for Evangelizing* (Emmaus Road, 2016) and a regular contributor to the *Catechetical Review*, *Homiletic and Pastoral Review*, and SpiritualDirection.com. He hosted the radio broadcast *Seeds of Truth*, which reached thousands of listeners in more than forty countries and can still be found as an iTunes podcast at joehollcraft.org.

Joseph earned his B.A. and M.A. from Franciscan University of Steubenville and received his Ph.D. from Graduate Theological Foundation, with studies completed at Oxford University. He has taught at the middle school, high school, and university levels.

Most importantly, Joseph is a devoted husband and father. He lives in Canal Fulton, Ohio, with his beautiful wife, Jackie, and their four children: Kolbe, Avila, Isaac, and Siena.

Sophia Institute

Sophia Institute is a nonprofit institution that seeks to nurture the spiritual, moral, and cultural life of souls and to spread the Gospel of Christ in conformity with the authentic teachings of the Roman Catholic Church.

Sophia Institute Press fulfills this mission by offering translations, reprints, and new publications that afford readers a rich source of the enduring wisdom of mankind.

Sophia Institute also operates the popular online resource CatholicExchange.com. *Catholic Exchange* provides world news from a Catholic perspective as well as daily devotionals and articles that will help readers to grow in holiness and live a life consistent with the teachings of the Church.

In 2013, Sophia Institute launched Sophia Institute for Teachers to renew and rebuild Catholic culture through service to Catholic education. With the goal of nurturing the spiritual, moral, and cultural life of souls, and an abiding respect for the role and work of teachers, we strive to provide materials and programs that are at once enlightening to the mind and ennobling to the heart; faithful and complete, as well as useful and practical.

Sophia Institute gratefully recognizes the Solidarity Association for preserving and encouraging the growth of our apostolate over the course of many years. Without their generous and timely support, this book would not be in your hands.

www.SophiaInstitute.com
www.CatholicExchange.com
www.SophiaInstituteforTeachers.org

Sophia Institute Press® is a registered trademark of Sophia Institute.
Sophia Institute is a tax-exempt institution as defined by the
Internal Revenue Code, Section 501(c)(3). Tax ID 22-2548708.